IDENTIFYING CHILDREN WITH SPECIAL NEEDS

Checklists

and

Action Plans

for

Teachers

GLYNIS HANNELL

CORWIN PRESS
A SAGE Publications Company
Thousand Oaks, California

For information:

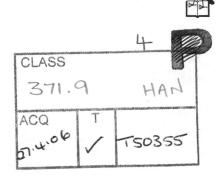

Corwin Press
A Sage Publications Company
2455 Teller Road
Thousand Oaks, California 91320
www.corwinpress.com

Sage Publications Ltd.
1 Oliver's Yard
55 City Road
London EC1Y 1SP
United Kingdom

Sage Publications India Pvt. Ltd.
B-42, Panchsheel Enclave
Post Box 4109
New Delhi 110 017 India

Printed in the United States of America

Library of Congress Cataloging-in-Publication Data

Hannell, Glynis.
Identifying children with special needs: Checklists and action plans for teachers /
Glynis Hannell.
     p. cm.
Includes bibliographical references and index.
ISBN 1-4129-1594-5 (cloth)—ISBN 1-4129-1595-3 (pbk.)
  1. Children with disabilities—Education. 2. Needs assessment. 3. Ability—Testing.
I. Title.
LC4019.H363 2006
371.9—dc22   2005014841

This book is printed on acid-free paper.

05   06   07   08   09   10   9 8 7 6 5 4 3 2 1

Developmental Editor:	Melinda Jane Burnette
Acquisitions Editor:	Kylee Liegl
Production Editor:	Laureen Shea
Copy Editor:	Julie Gwin
Typesetter:	C&M Digitals (P) Ltd.
Proofreader:	Christine Dahlin
Indexer:	Michael Ferreira
Cover Designer:	Rose Storey

IDENTIFYING CHILDREN WITH SPECIAL NEEDS

Contents

Acknowledgments

Corwin Press gratefully acknowledges the contributions of the following reviewers:

Judith Smock
Fifth-Grade Teacher
Clark Elementary School
Erie, PA

Jorrie MacKenzie
NBCT
Los Angeles USD
Los Angeles, CA

Laura Seese
Educational Psychologist
Educational Advancement
    Associates
Burlington, CT

John La Londe
Director
Marin SELPA
San Rafael, CA

Jo Bellanti
Director of Special Education
Shelby County Schools
Bartlett, TN

Robert W. Pickett
First-Grade Teacher
Marion Elementary School
Sheridan, IN

Mary Apple
Special Education Director
Union Baker ESD
Baker City, OR

Carrie Carpenter
Oregon Teacher of the Year 2003
Hugh Hartman Middle School
Redmond, OR

Susan M. Dannemiller
Director of Special Education and
    Pupil Services
School District of Grafton
Grafton, WI

About the Author

 **Glynis Hannell** has a BA (Hons.) in Psychology and an MSc in Child Development, both from London University. She has worked as an educational and developmental psychologist in education departments, child health organizations, and child development units. She has also lectured in child development at the University of South Australia. She is currently a consultant psychologist working with children and adolescents with special needs, their teachers, their parents and caregivers, and other professionals. She contributes to professional conferences and professional inservice training programs.

Introduction

Background to the Checklists

This manual is designed to assist teachers in deciding whether to refer a student for special education assessment. It includes 17 checklists that were developed in consultation with pediatricians, child psychiatrists, psychologists, speech pathologists, classroom and special education teachers, parents and caregivers, and organizations dealing with specific difficulties or disorders. The checklists are consistent (if applicable) with the *Diagnostic and Statistical Manual of Mental Disorders* (American Psychiatric Association, 1994, 4th ed.; *DSM-IV*), which is recognized internationally as the standard diagnostic reference. In the United States, special education services are provided in accordance with 13 categories enumerated in the Individuals with Disabilities Education Act (IDEA) and a 14th category, "Developmental Delay," which is used for children ages 3 through 9 at the discretion of the state or local education agency. If applicable, the checklists in this manual are grouped according to the IDEA categories. The checklists are also consistent with other reputable sources of information on disabilities.

For the convenience of professionals, several checklists are included that are either not in *DSM-IV* or are not IDEA categories. Giftedness, Low Self-Esteem, Child Abuse, and Immaturity are not *DSM-IV* categories. Giftedness, Low Self-Esteem, Child Abuse, Immaturity, and Developmental Coordination and Dyspraxia are not IDEA special education disability categories.

The checklists are intended as decision aids for the convenience of professionals working with a range of students, not all of whom may be eligible for services under special education programs such as IDEA, but who nevertheless have special needs in the classroom. Each checklist is divided into subcategories so that observations often fall into a pattern. These patterns help the professional understand the particular nature of the child's or adolescent's difficulties or special needs.

A WORD ABOUT IDEA

IDEA is the main U.S. federal special education program. It requires that all students with disabilities be provided a free, appropriate education in the student's least restrictive environment. Through IDEA, the federal government provides funding to states to help defray the expense of providing special education services. States must report to the federal government the number of students receiving services. The federal Department of Education, in turn, reports these numbers to Congress in an annual report on the implementation of IDEA. For both state and federal reporting purposes, students in each state are counted in one of 13 disability categories or under the category "Developmental Delay" (see the list on the following page).

The more general category of Developmental Delay is used by states for students ages 3 through 9 who show delays in physical development, cognitive development, communication development, social or emotional development, or adaptive development. This category allows states to provide special education and related services to students, according to state definitions and as measured by appropriate instruments, without classifying them in one of the more specific federal disability categories. The Developmental Delay category is defined by the state (if the state chooses to use it), and local education agencies may choose to use it or not. If the category is used, it may be used in conjunction with the other disability categories. For example, if a student is classified as having a Hearing Impairment, he or she may also be classified as having a Developmental Delay if the state definition for Developmental Delay is met.

The Developmental Delay category is used by states for students who clearly have learning problems, but whose problems do not unmistakably fall into one of the 13 disability categories. In this way, states can avoid labeling students whose learning problems may be more ambiguous.

Even for students who are classified in one of the disability categories, special education services must address all of the child's special education and related services needs and must be based on the identified needs of the child, not the child's disability category.

As you review the IDEA disability categories, you may notice that some of the categories are not represented in the checklists in this manual. These categories are Deaf-Blindness, Deafness, Hearing Impairment, Multiple Disabilities, Orthopedic Impairment, Traumatic Brain Injury, and Visual Impairment (including Blindness).

Disabilities in these categories often would be identified by medical professionals or by preschool and school health screenings. It is likely that the school district would be aware of the student's condition before he or she is assigned to the general education class. Because this manual is designed to aid general education teachers in making decisions about whether students need referral for special education assessment, these categories are not included in the checklists provided here.

However, some students who have conditions such as Hearing or Visual Impairments are not identified by medical professionals or by screenings, and they can present a confusing picture to classroom teachers trying to address their learning problems. It is not always apparent, for example, that a child's trouble learning to read may be due to a Visual Impairment, or that failure to follow the teacher's directions may be due to the fact that the child cannot hear what is said. To address this possibility, this manual provides "warning signs" for classroom teachers to help them consider whether an unfound disability of this nature is causing learning problems. In addition, items about these conditions are included in the checklists where relevant.

IDEA DISABILITY CATEGORIES SEC. 300.7 (20 U.S.C. 1401[3][A] AND [B]; 1401 [26])

- Autism
- Deaf-Blindness
- Deafness
- Emotional Disturbance
- Hearing Impairment
- Mental Retardation
- Multiple Disabilities
- Orthopedic Impairment
- Other Health Impairment (e.g., Asthma, Attention-Deficit Disorder or Attention-Deficit/Hyperactivity Disorder, Diabetes, Epilepsy, Heart Condition, Hemophilia, Lead Poisoning, Leukemia, Nephritis, Rheumatic Fever, Sickle Cell Anemia)
- Specific Learning Disability (e.g., Perceptual Disabilities, Brain Injury, Minimal Brain Dysfunction, Dyslexia, Developmental Aphasia)
- Speech or Language Impairment
- Traumatic Brain Injury
- Visual Impairment including Blindness
- Developmental Delay*

REFERENCE

American Psychiatric Association. (1994). *Diagnostic and statistical manual of mental disorders* (4th ed.). Washington, DC: Author.

---

* Use of the Developmental Delay category is discussed in the previous text.

THE SPECIAL EDUCATION DISABILITY IDENTIFICATION PROCESS

Every professional working with children and adolescents will sometimes have concerns regarding a particular student's learning or behavioral difficulties. In this situation, the professional may need to adjust the student's program, adapt classroom procedures, and make a decision about whether to seek further advice. This book of checklists can be a valuable tool in this process.

All teachers continuously observe their students, and such observations are the source of valuable information about the student's individual needs. Other professionals will also use continuous observation as part of their professional assessment of the children or adolescents with whom they work. Using an appropriate checklist, the professional can organize his or her observations into a systematic framework. This structured record of observations is a valuable tool in identifying students with special needs and an important basis for planning an appropriate response to the student's observed difficulties or special characteristics.

Table 1.1 provides an overview of the decision making process and the ways the checklists can be helpful.

Table 1.1   Referring Students for Special Education Eligibility: Investigation and
Problem-Solving Process

Step 1. General education teacher notices that student is having problems. Observes
the student to identify and describe the entire constellation of the student's problems.
Considers whether cultural differences, lack of language proficiency, or inadequate
prior learning may play a part in the student's difficulties. Tries different instructional
approaches to teach the student; notices what works and what doesn't. (If student's
learning problems are ameliorated, end of process.)

Step 2. Teacher finds that student still has some problems in specific areas and comes
to wonder if the student may need special education services. Observes, describes, and
delineates all of the student's problem areas.

Step 3. Teacher completes the reference charts and checklists to see if the student
shows a pattern of problems corresponding to any of the patterns given in the checklists or charts. Teacher keeps in mind that each student may have a different constellation of problems.

Step 4A. If teacher does not find pattern, teacher uses school resources to try to make
sense of and address student's problems. Teacher tries alternative instruction. If successful, teacher continues to use school resources to ensure that student does well.
Teacher provides information about instructional strategies used and the way the
student learns to future teachers.

Step 4B. If the review of charts and checklists indicates that a pattern may exist, teacher
uses appropriate checklists to collect and organize information. Consults with parents
and specialists; may use checklists as interview schedule or may have parents fill out
checklist. Uses action plans to identify instructional strategies that may help the student
learn. Teacher documents the instructional strategies tried and their results.
If strategies work, teacher monitors student closely. If strategies do not work, teacher
requests intervention team meeting.

Step 5. Teacher requests intervention team meeting. (Intervention team meeting may
also be requested by parents.) Teacher prepares for meeting using checklists to organize
information about the student, gathering other information as listed on page.

Step 6. Intervention team meeting is held. Follow-up meeting is scheduled.

Step 7. Follow-up intervention team meeting is held. Decision is made to refer student
for special services or not. If strategies have been successful, referral is deferred and
student is monitored closely. If strategies are not successful, referral is made.

Step 8. Referral review meeting is held. All information needed for an Individualized
Education Program (IEP) meeting is collected.

Step 9. IEP meeting is held. IEP is developed. Teacher receives copy of the IEP and works
with student's instructional team.

USING THE CHECKLISTS

Who Should Use the Checklists?

The checklists are designed to be used by professionals working with
children or adolescents. However, under the direction of the professional, the

checklists can also be used by parents to record their observations of their own child or adolescent. The importance of information from parents cannot be overstated. Parents see their child in an environment different from the school environment, and they can provide crucial information about how or whether the child's difficulties present themselves outside of school. In addition, parents can provide insights about how cultural differences may be affecting the child's school behavior. Children's behavior can appear very different when seen from the perspective of the parents, and a wise teacher will make every effort to understand that perspective.

In some situations, several people (such as the student's teacher, the parent, or a therapist) each complete a copy of the same checklist. Once all the individual checklists have been completed, the results can be transposed onto a single checklist (using color coding to differentiate the origin of each item). In this way, points of similarity and comparisons between different observers or different situations can be clarified.

Using School Resources (Table 1.1, Step 4A)

If the teacher has concerns about the student that are not ameliorated by his or her initial attempts, school resources can be an invaluable aid in clarifying students' problems. Such resources might include informal conversations with the student's previous teacher, a master teacher, a special education teacher, the school's counselor, the assistant principal, or the principal. In addition, all developed countries will have an advisory and assessment service that provides support to general educators who have specific concerns about an individual student's learning or behavioral difficulties. In some countries, there may be a special unit or centrally based advisory service that has the responsibility for providing schools with services for special-needs students.

The U.S. model would be similar to the approach used in many other countries. In the United States, the starting point for identification of special needs students is a school-based team known as the intervention team, the pre-referral team, the teacher assistance team, the preplacement team, or something similar. This committee will usually be a classroom teacher's first point of reference when seeking additional help for an individual student's difficulties. These types of consultation not only provide the general education teacher with more information, they can validate his or her concerns, provide support, and give the teacher greater confidence in his or her decisions about the student and the student's instruction.

Completing the Checklists (Table 1.1, Step 4B)

Chapter 2 describes how to select the appropriate checklists for a particular student.

The checklists can be used for children or adolescents between the ages of 4 and 18. Each checklist is accompanied by descriptions of the characteristics and causes of the disorder, a list of similar conditions, other conditions that may accompany the disorder, and a set of action plans for teachers.

The checklists help make sense of what has been observed. The items often prompt consideration of other behaviors that may be relevant but not previously noted. From this basis, the professional, perhaps in consultation with colleagues, can begin to evaluate the significance of the information that has been observed and recorded.

Different Ways of Using the Checklists

Although they are primarily intended for the classroom teacher as an aid for decisions about whether to refer a student for special education assessment, the checklists can also be used in discussing the student with specialists and teams and as an interview schedule when talking with parents, other educators, or specialists.

When the checklists are used to summarize information for other educators and specialists, they provide a concise description of the teacher's concerns about the student. In addition, they present information in a format that coordinates with internationally accepted diagnostic criteria for developmental and psychological disorders in children and adolescents.

When the checklists are used as an interview schedule, the professional sits together with a colleague or parent talking through the items one by one. This gives direction and structure to an interview or discussion, ensuring that a wide spectrum of possible concerns can be explored.

Interpreting the Results of the Checklists

All children are unique, and we need to respect their developmental and cultural diversity. Professionals, parents, and caregivers filling in these checklists need to recognize that each individual child may be quite different from the norm and yet have no disorders or difficulties at all. Observed behaviors may be reflections of a child's unique personality, learned behaviors, or cultural differences.

Each checklist clearly states, "It is important to remember that many conditions have similar characteristics and that specialist assessment is necessary for formal diagnosis." This applies to all of the conditions covered by this set of checklists.

The items in the checklists are not intended to be definitive diagnostic criteria; rather, they are records of observed behaviors that may indicate that the student has a disorder, difficulty, or special need. Professionals need to be open minded about the origin of the observed behaviors, especially at the early stages of identification and assessment, when more information needs to be gathered.

In the United States, the Individuals with Disabilities Education Act (IDEA) prevents children from being identified with a disability on the basis of (a) lack of instruction in reading or math or (b) limited English proficiency. This means that teachers and specialists must consider whether the child's learning problems are due to these conditions as opposed to representing a true disability. It is important to note that such disadvantages as lack of instruction or limited English proficiency can occur in parallel with a disability or disorder, so that both might be present at the same time.

Obviously, a student who frequently shows the behaviors specified in a checklist is more likely to need further assessment and investigation than one who is generally rated as seldom showing these behaviors.

Professionals should remember that these checklists are used for preliminary screening, not diagnosis. If in doubt, always seek further advice from colleagues with specialist expertise. Your completed checklist is a quick and easy way to pass on information about the student and the characteristics that you have observed.

When several people complete the same checklist, it is not unusual for different people to rate the items differently. One teacher may have concerns about concentration, another may not. A parent may be extremely concerned about a particular behavior that is never observed at school. The variations in ratings can, in themselves, provide very useful information for professionals, reflecting the complexity and diversity of the individual student's special needs in different settings or in different circumstances.

Taking Further Action

If the teacher sees from the checklist that the student has a pattern of difficulties in some areas but no difficulties at all in others, planning can immediately be undertaken to work with the student's unique profile. The action plans included with the checklists provide alternative instructional strategies that the teacher can use to help the student learn. The strategies used with the student and their results should be documented by the teacher.

However, teachers must always use their own judgment and take further action if they believe that this is necessary. For example, the child or adolescent may only be displaying one or two behaviors rated as 3 and yet the teacher believes there is a serious problem. In this case, a referral for further consideration should be initiated immediately.

*Implement appropriate action plans and monitor
carefully if any of the following criteria are met.*

- Any item is rated 3 (severe, frequently observed, strongly applies).
- 3 or more items are rated 2 (moderate, often observed, certainly applies).
- 10 or more items are rated 1 (mild, sometimes observed, applies to some extent).
- Your overall level of concern is moderate.

If these interventions help the student learn successfully, the teacher should monitor the student closely and should be sure that future teachers receive information about the strategies used and the way the student learns. If the teacher's preliminary intervention plans do not seem to be resolving the difficulties, then the teacher can use the information to arrange for further investigation.

Often, the completed checklist adds weight to the teacher's suspicions that the student has special educational needs and needs further assessment. At this point, the teacher should request a meeting of the intervention team (Table 1.1, Step 5). For IDEA requirements in meetings related to special education eligibility, see Table 1.2.

Table 1.2   Individuals with Disabilities Education Act (IDEA) Requirements Regarding Meetings

Meeting	Purpose	Comments
Intervention Team Meeting	To provide specialist support to the teacher's attempts to address student's problems in the general education classroom. To help ensure that student's problems are not due to limited English proficiency, cultural differences, or lack of instruction in English or math.	This meeting occurs before a referral decision is made and does not come under the auspices of IDEA.
Follow-Up Intervention Team Meeting	To review the effects of intervention strategies tried in the general education classroom. To determine if student should be referred for special education assessment. If so, to plan and order evaluation of the student's learning problems.	Informed, written parental consent is required before evaluation. Evaluation must address the extent to which the child can be involved in and progress in the general curriculum. Observations by the child's teachers and related services providers are required.
Referral Review Meeting	To review and interpret all available information regarding the student and determine if additional evaluation data is needed. To provide all evaluation information needed for the Individualized Education Program (IEP) meeting.	Parent input is required in interpreting evaluation data for the purposes of determining a child's eligibility for special education.
IEP Meeting	To develop the student's IEP to address his or her learning needs. To translate problems into learning needs and to plan and document interventions. To assign roles and responsibilities to staff, family members, and advocates. Regular education teacher and parents will receive copies of the IEP.	IDEA requires that the IEP team include: • the parents; • at least one of the child's general education teachers; • at least one special education teacher or special education service provider; • a public agency representative who is qualified to provide or supervise the provision of specially designed instruction and who is knowledgeable about the general education curriculum and the availability of resources of the public agency; • an individual who can interpret the instructional implications of evaluation results; • other individuals at the discretion of the parents or the agency who have knowledge of or special expertise regarding the child, including related services personnel as appropriate; • representatives of other agencies that may be involved in paying for services needed by the child; • other qualified professionals; and • if appropriate, the child.

Note: Overall, IDEA requires that the parents of a child with a disability are members of any group that makes decisions on the educational placement of the child.

Immediately initiate the referral process and implement
appropriate actions plans if any of the following criteria are met.

- 4 or more items are rated 3 (severe, frequently observed, strongly applies).
- 10 or more items are rated 2 (moderate, often observed, certainly applies).
- Your overall concern is high.

Requesting and Preparing for an Intervention Team Meeting (Table 1.1, Step 5)

Once the teacher has decided to request an intervention team meeting, it will be important to present information to describe current concerns with regard to the student in a clear and concise manner. In the event that the student's parents have requested the meeting, the teacher can use this information to prepare for the meeting or to work with the parents to clarify their concerns. For both teacher and parents, the checklists can be used to identify specific areas of concern, giving the information in a succinct and organized format. The checklists may also bring out other, related concerns that might not be spontaneously recalled during unstructured discussions during the meeting.

Since the general education teacher will be working with the student's parents throughout the eligibility process and the student's subsequent instruction, it is important to establish a professional, cordial, and communicative working relationship with them from the beginning. IDEA makes some specific requirements regarding communications with parents (see Table 1.3).

Table 1.3   Individuals with Disabilities Education Act (IDEA) Requirements Regarding Communication With Parents

Written notice must be given to the parents of a child with a disability a reasonable time before the school proposes (or refuses) to *identify, evaluate, or change the educational placement of* the child. This written notice must be provided in the native language of the parent or other mode of communication used by the parent, unless it is clearly not feasible to do so. (If the native language or other mode of communication of the parent is not a written language, the school must take steps to ensure that the notice is translated orally or by other means to the parent in his or her native language or other mode of communication, that the parent understands the content of the notice, and that there is written evidence that these two requirements have been met.)

The state education agency must fully inform parents that they have detailed policies and procedures to ensure confidentiality of any personally identifiable information collected, used, or maintained.

Informed, written parental consent is required before evaluation. Parents have the right to receive a copy of the evaluation report and the paperwork about the child's eligibility for special education services.

(Continued)

Table 1.3 (Continued)

Parental input is required in interpreting evaluation data for the purposes of determining a child's eligibility for special education.

If the child has been found not eligible for special education services, the school must tell parents in writing and explain why the student was found not eligible.

Parents must be informed that they may issue an invitation to the [Individualized Education Program] IEP meeting to other individuals who have knowledge of or special expertise about the child (for example, an advocate for the family, their religious leader, etc.).

Schools must take whatever action necessary to ensure that the parent understands the proceedings of the IEP meeting, including arranging for an interpreter for parents with deafness or whose native language is other than English.

Parents must receive a free copy of the IEP, whether they request it or not.

Note: Parents have the right to see their child's school records.

The teacher will need to assemble as much information as possible about the student. Documentation that can be useful to take to the meeting with the committee may include any of the following:

- Basic demographic information with regard to the student (age, gender, home address, known medical conditions, sensory status, family structure)
- Anecdotal reports of typical behaviors that have caused concern
- Running records of teacher observations of the student
- Information with regard to the frequency, duration, and intensity of any behaviors that are causing concern
- Copies of previous medical, psychological, or other reports on the student
- Copies of previous school reports
- Records of any previous meetings held with regard to the student
- Information from other teaching staff who have contact with the student
- Samples of the student's work
- Student's home-school communication book if used/relevant
- Results of any classroom or external tests that the students may have taken recently
- Information on parents' concerns
- Information on how the student sees his or her own difficulties
- Any reference materials that have already been collected with regard to the student's special needs
- Details of strategies that have already been tried and the outcomes of these strategies
- Information on any intervention strategies that the parents have initiated
- Copies of any checklists that the student's teachers have completed
- Copies of any checklists that the student's parents or caregivers have completed

The Intervention Team Meeting

The purpose of the meeting is to discuss the student's difficulties and consider what intervention strategies might be appropriate. The information presented in checklist format can facilitate a good match between the pattern of difficulties that the student is experiencing and the intervention strategies that are planned. In this way, the chances of successful intervention are increased.

During the meeting, there will also be a review of the instructional strategies that teachers and parents have tried with this student and the results of those strategies. The action plan descriptions in this manual can help the teacher present this information, along with the results. At the meeting, a decision may be made to implement more of these intervention strategies, to use different strategies, or to modify the selected strategies.

If asked to do so, the general education teacher should be prepared to help evaluate the English-language proficiency of children whose native language is not English. IDEA requires this assessment during evaluation, along with an assessment in the child's native language, to distinguish language proficiency from disability needs.

Some states in the United States require that a minimum of two intervention strategies are tried before any referral can be made for further assessment. Teachers should check their state's special education policies to see if this applies. The classroom teacher will be responsible for keeping adequate records of the process of intervention and for recording the student's response to the changes that have been initiated.

The agreement to put specified strategies into place will need to be documented by a member of the committee. The classroom teacher must retain a copy of these agreed-on intervention strategies.

As well as suggesting intervention strategies, the committee may also suggest that one or more of the checklists in this book should be completed to provide additional information with regard to the student's difficulties. If so, this should be completed as soon as possible to provide a snapshot view of the student before intervention is started. The checklist can then be completed again at the end of the period of intervention to identify any changes that may have occurred.

The committee may also suggest that a checklist that has already been completed should be filled in again at the end of the trial period of intervention, to see if any changes or progress can be identified.

If parents have not been previously informed of teacher's concerns, they must be contacted and told about the student's perceived difficulties and the action that is being taken by the classroom teacher. Looking over a completed checklist can be a very effective way of conveying the exact nature of concerns to the student's parents.

A follow-up meeting will be arranged (usually about a month after the intervention strategies have been implemented) to evaluate the effectiveness of the interventions that have been put into action. Before the meeting, the parents will need to know the outcomes of the intervention strategies that have been tried. They will also need to know that another meeting is scheduled and that they will be told the outcome of that meeting.

If the situation is critical, the trial run of classroom intervention strategies may be bypassed and an immediate special education referral made.

Follow-Up Intervention Team Meeting: The Decision to Refer or Not (Table 1.1, Step 6)

At the follow-up meeting, the classroom teacher will need to present:

- A detailed record of the interventions that have been tried
- A detailed record of the student's responses to those interventions

If available, the following should also be presented:

- Any new information that has been obtained (e.g., medical reports, reference materials, etc.)
- Any changes in demographic details (e.g., change in family circumstances that may impact the effectiveness of the interventions)
- Any further checklists that have been completed during the intervention period
- Records of any significant new difficulties or concerns that have emerged since the previous meeting

If the intervention strategies that have been used have been effective, then the committee will probably agree that these approaches should continue and that the special education referral should be deferred for the time being. Additional intervention strategies may be suggested and agreed on.

Parents will need to be informed that the meeting has concluded that the intervention strategies have been effective and that they will therefore continue. Parents should be told that no special education referral will be made at this time (see Table 1.3).

If the intervention strategies have not been successful, then the committee may decide on a special education referral. Parents will need to be informed of this decision. Explain to them that this is a formal procedure of review, leading to the development of an assessment plan, which in turn may lead to an Individualized Education Program (IEP).

Making a Referral (Table 1.1, Step 7)

Once the decision to make a special education referral has been made, the appropriate Referral for Special Education form should be completed. Information about the student will be recorded and details of previous intervention strategies will be required.

The form will be signed by the classroom teacher and countersigned by the responsible administrator. The form is then forwarded to the school psychologist and the special education staff.

Parents will need to be informed that the referral has been made (see Table 1.3). A date for a referral review meeting will then be set. Parents should be informed of the time and place of this meeting so that they can attend.

Checklists not previously completed can be used at this stage to facilitate collating further information prior to the referral review meeting. For example, parents might be asked to complete a checklist to help them organize their information about their child. Teachers might refer to the reference charts in Chapter 2 and consider using checklists that were not previously used, but that might relate to the student's difficulties.

Checklists can be forwarded to the convener, prior to the meeting, and slated for consideration by the referral meeting team.

The Referral Review Meeting (Table 1.1, Step 8)

People attending this meeting will include:

- The classroom teacher
- The school principal
- The school psychologist
- Special education staff (the particular people attending will depend on the student's presenting difficulties; for example, an Emotional or Behavioral Disorder teacher will attend if the issues relate to the student's behavior, an Autism Spectrum Disorder teacher will attend if this is the probable disorder, etc.)
- Parents and caregivers

This group of people will discuss the student's difficulties prior to completion of the referral review form. The referral form requires information across 10 different domains. The checklists can be used to provide additional information which can be forwarded with the referral review form.

Outcome of the Referral Review Meeting

The participants will discuss all available information and then decide on an assessment plan. This will be documented in a notice of education assessment/ reassessment plan. Permission from parents must be obtained before the assessment process can commence.

The Assessment

The special education staff will decide on who undertakes the actual assessment. A range of formal and informal assessment tools may be used depending on the presenting problems. The assessments will ascertain whether a student meets the criteria for a special education disability category. Then an IEP team, including the general education teacher and parents, will work toward the development of an appropriate IEP.

The checklists can be used as a valuable tool in organizing observations made on the basis of the student's behavior in typical, day-to-day situations.

The clustering of observations into categories can help the special education staff ascertain the precise nature and pattern of the student's difficulties, which in turn helps relate the IEP to the student's particular difficulties.

REFERENCES

Harwell, J. M. (2000). *Complete learning disabilities handbook.* San Francisco: Jossey-Bass.

Jean, M. (2000). *A manual of special education law for educators and parents.* Naples, FL: Morgen.

Maanum, J. L. (2004). *The general educator's guide to special education* (2nd ed.). Minnetonka, MN: Peytral.

Pierangelo, R. A. (2002). *Survival guide for the special education teacher.* San Francisco: Jossey-Bass.

Shelton, C. F., & Pollingue, A. B. (2000). *The exceptional teacher's handbook.* Thousand Oaks, CA: Corwin.

WHICH CHECKLIST TO USE?

This chapter provides a set of charts to help you decide which checklists give the fullest coverage of the behavioral or learning characteristics that have been observed. The charts cover the following categories:

- Motivation and concentration difficulties
- Communication difficulties
- Social and behavioral difficulties
- Learning difficulties

HOW TO USE THE CHARTS

It is a good idea to make a copy of the charts before you begin and work from those copies. Thinking about the student's learning problems and behaviors in class, look at the behaviors shown across the top of each chart, and check those that are of concern with this student. When you have finished selecting the appropriate columns on all four checklists, look down the columns to see which boxes are filled in. Put a check in those that are shaded (dark or light gray on the chart), corresponding to the columns you have selected.

When you have finished, look across the rows for the disabling condition that has the largest number of checkmarks, and use the checklist for that condition.

Remember that a student may have more than one type of special educational need. Several disorders are known to occur together (for instance, Specific Learning Disability is strongly associated with Attention-Deficit Disorder and vice versa).

Other disorders may occur together just by chance, for instance, a gifted student might also be anxious or depressed. You may need to use two or more checklists if you suspect that the student has a complex pattern of difficulties.

SCENARIO ILLUSTRATING USE OF THE CHARTS

John is a student in Mrs. Carter's third-grade class. Although her students are at various levels in reading, Mrs. Carter has noticed that John is way behind. It is almost midyear, and John only knows the basic Dolch sightword vocabulary. He will learn a new vocabulary word one day, and then forget it the next. He seems to only recognize the words he learned by rote.

Mrs. Carter has also noticed that John has trouble pronouncing words of more than two syllables. His spelling and writing are poor.

John is a quiet child who does not make friends easily. In class, he sits silently and does not volunteer answers or participate much in class discussions. At recess, he plays with one or two friends (usually the same ones every day) and seldom participates in group games.

Mrs. Carter is primarily concerned because of John's reading difficulties, but she also fears that he will fall farther and farther behind because of his lack of engagement in class.

Mrs. Carter looks at the reference chart for motivation and concentration difficulties and checks "Slow to start or complete general classwork," "Seems to be in a world of his own," "Work is messy—looks careless," and "Student lacks motivation toward schoolwork." On the chart for communication difficulties, she checks "Reluctant to speak in some situations" and "Has difficulties pronouncing words." Only one category is checked on the social and behavioral difficulties chart. It is "Has few if any friends."

On the chart for learning difficulties, she checks "Is not up to age standard in literacy," "Inaccurate spelling," and "Poor handwriting and bookwork."

When Mrs. Carter checks the shaded boxes in the columns she has chosen, she sees that most of them are in the row labeled "Language Impairment." This is the checklist she uses to help her make decisions about getting further support for John.

MOTIVATION AND CONCENTRATION DIFFICULTIES:

Observations and Possible Diagnostic Categories

Legend: ■ = Very strong possibility · ▨ = Strong possibility · □ = Possibility · * = Student unlikely to be in this situation

	Disruptive in class	Slow to start or complete general classwork	Does not complete homework properly	Complains of being bored in school	Lacks confidence in own ability	Seems to be in a world of his or her own	Work is messy—looks careless	Student lacks motivation toward schoolwork	Says the work is too hard	Impulsive, does not stop and think
Autism	■	*	*			■	■		*	
Asperger Syndrome	▨				▨	▨	▨			
Anxiety Disorder		▨			■				▨	
Selective Mutism										
Depression		▨	▨	■		▨		■	▨	
Conduct Disorder	■		■							
Oppositional Defiant Disorder	■		■							
Mental Retardation	▨	■	■	▨			■		■	
Attention-Deficit Disorder (Inattentive Type)		■	■	■	■	■	■	■	■	
Attention-Deficit/Hyperactivity Disorder	■	■	■	■	▨		■	■		■
Tourette's Syndrome	■									
Specific Learning Disability		■	■		▨		■	▨	■	
Speech or Language Impairment		▨			▨					
Giftedness	▨			■		▨				
Immaturity									▨	
Low Self-Esteem					■				▨	
Child Abuse	▨				▨	▨		▨		
Developmental Coordination/Dyspraxia							■			

* = Student unlikely to be in this situation · ▨ = Strong possibility · ■ = Very strong possibility · □ = Possibility

COMMUNICATION DIFFICULTIES:

Observations and Possible Diagnostic Categories

	Cannot use language to communicate effectively	Speaks "like a professor"	Poor at reading non-verbal language	Reluctant to speak in some situations	Makes inappropriate noises	Has difficulties pronouncing some words	Has difficulties remembering instructions	Gets muddled when trying to recount an event	Restless and inattentive when others are speaking	Suspected of having a hearing difficulty
Autism	Very strong		Very strong		Very strong		*	*	Very strong	Strong
Asperger Syndrome		Very strong	Very strong							
Anxiety Disorder				Strong						
Selective Mutism				Very strong						
Depression										Very strong
Conduct Disorder										
Oppositional Defiant Disorder										
Mental Retardation	Very strong		Very strong		Strong	Strong	Very strong	Very strong	Very strong	
Attention-Deficit Disorder (Inattentive Type)							Very strong		Very strong	Very strong
Attention-Deficit/Hyperactivity Disorder					Very strong				Very strong	
Tourette's Syndrome					Very strong					
Specific Learning Disability						Strong	Very strong			
Speech or Language Impairment	Very strong			Very strong		Very strong	Very strong	Very strong	Very strong	Very strong
Giftedness		Very strong								
Immaturity										
Low Self-Esteem										
Child Abuse										
Developmental Coordination/Dyspraxia						Very strong				

Legend:
- [*] Student unlikely to be in this situation
- Very strong possibility
- Strong possibility
- Possibility

SOCIAL AND BEHAVIORAL DIFFICULTIES:

Observations and Possible Diagnostic Categories

	Has few if any friends	Easily annoyed/ aggressive	Poor empathy with others	Does not obey requests or instructions	Easily upset if things do not go his or her way	Overly dependent on adults	Bullies or harasses other students	Rigid/obsessional	Has odd or unusual interests	Sexually inappropriate behavior	Poor self-control	Easily upset and worried
Autism	■		■	■	■			■	■		■	▨
Asperger Syndrome	■		■	□	■			■	■			■
Anxiety Disorder					▨	▨		▨				■
Selective Mutism								▨				▨
Depression		■			■							■
Conduct Disorder	■	■	■	■	■		■			■	■	
Oppositional Defiant Disorder	■	■	■	■	▨		■			■	■	
Mental Retardation	▨	▨		▨	▨	▨				▨	▨	▨
Attention-Deficit Disorder (Inattentive Type)				▨								
Attention-Deficit/ Hyperactivity Disorder		▨									▨	
Tourette's Syndrome								▨				▨
Specific Learning Disability												
Speech or Language Impairment				■								
Giftedness									■			
Immaturity						▨	▨					▨
Low Self-Esteem												
Child Abuse		▨				▨				■		▨
Developmental Coordination/Dyspraxia												

■ Very strong possibility   ▨ Strong possibility   □ Possibility

LEARNING DIFFICULTIES:

Observations and Possible Diagnostic Categories

	Is not up to age standard in literacy	Is not up to age standard in numeracy	Reading comprehension exceeds reading accuracy	Reading accuracy exceeds reading comprehension	Inaccurate spelling	Poor handwriting and bookwork	Effort not reflected in results	Dislikes reading or writing	Written language is poorly structured	Difficulty learning times tables
Autism	Very strong	Very strong		Very strong		Strong		*		*
Asperger Syndrome				Very strong		Strong				
Anxiety Disorder										
Selective Mutism										
Depression										
Conduct Disorder										
Oppositional Defiant Disorder										
Mental Retardation	Very strong	Very strong		Strong	Very strong	Very strong	Very strong	Very strong	Very strong	Very strong
Attention-Deficit Disorder (Inattentive Type)								Very strong		
Attention-Deficit/ Hyperactivity Disorder						Strong		Very strong		
Tourette's Syndrome										
Specific Learning Disability	Very strong	Very strong	Very strong		Very strong	Very strong	Very strong	Very strong	Very strong	Very strong
Speech or Language Impairment	Very strong	Very strong		Strong	Strong		Strong	Very strong	Very strong	
Giftedness										
Immaturity						Strong				
Low Self-Esteem										
Child Abuse										
Developmental Coordination/Dyspraxia						Very strong	Very strong			

[*] Student unlikely to be in this situation	▦ Strong possibility
■ Very strong possibility	▢ Possibility

AUTISM SPECTRUM DISORDERS (ASD)

Two checklists are included in this section:

- Autism
- Asperger Syndrome

DEFINITION OF AUTISM: INDIVIDUALS WITH DISABILITIES EDUCATION ACT (IDEA)

Autism means a developmental disability significantly affecting verbal and nonverbal communication and social interaction, generally evident before age 3, that adversely affects a child's educational performance. Other characteristics often associated with autism are engagement in repetitive activities and stereotyped movements, resistance to environmental change or change in daily routines, and unusual responses to sensory experiences. The term does not apply if a child's educational performance is adversely affected primarily because the child has an emotional disturbance. . . .

A child who manifests the characteristics of "Autism" after age 3 could be diagnosed as having "Autism" if the [above] criteria are satisfied. (Sec. 300.7)

HOW TO USE THE CHECKLISTS

Complete the Checklist

Fill in the administrative details at the top of the form.

Consider each item in turn. Record your subjective evaluation of the extent to which that item applies to the student.

Add any additional comments or qualifications in the space provided at the end of the questionnaire.

Interpret the Checklist

The checklist is a screening instrument, and the ratings that you have selected reflect your observations of the child or adolescent. The more items that apply to a child or adolescent, and the more frequently these items have been observed, the more likely it is that the child or adolescent has an Autism Spectrum Disorder. However, it is important to remember that several other conditions have similar characteristics and that specialist assessment is necessary for formal diagnosis.

For your information, descriptions of the disorders, similar conditions, and conditions that may accompany the disorder are provided.

Decide Whether to Refer for Further Assessment

The checklists will help you to decide whether to refer the student for further assessment. Guidelines are given on pages 5 and 7 for interpreting the rating scales.

Look at the Subcategories of the Checklist

The subcategories will help you to isolate any specific areas of difficulty and plan appropriate intervention strategies targeted to the student's individual needs. The action plans that follow will help to give you some practical ideas on intervention strategies.

THE AUTISM CHECKLIST

Glynis Hannell, BA (Hons.), MSc Registered Psychologist

Student's name _____ Date _____ Student's age _____

Name of person completing checklist _____

Relationship to student _____

Each item should be checked off using the following rating scale:

0 Not at all, does not apply
1 Mild, sometimes observed, applies to some extent
2 Moderate, often observed, certainly applies
3 Severe, frequently observed, strongly applies

*Please use **0** to indicate that an item has been considered and does not apply. If the **0** is not checked, it is not clear if the item has been overlooked.*

Difficulties with nonverbal communication

Has limited use of eye contact to express feelings	0	1	2	3
Has limited understanding of or response to eye contact	0	1	2	3
Has limited use of gesture or physical touching to express feelings or wishes	0	1	2	3
Does not seem to understand gestures or physical touching from others	0	1	2	3
Does not show much facial expression	0	1	2	3
Does not find it easy to "read" facial expression in others	0	1	2	3
Does not readily exchange social smiles	0	1	2	3
Does not often enjoy physical contact (e.g., cuddles, hugs, or tickles)	0	1	2	3
Is a poor judge of social distance; stands too close or too far away	0	1	2	3

Difficulties with social and emotional empathy

Does not seem to understand or "connect" with other people's feelings	0	1	2	3
Does not often bring or point out objects of interest for others to see	0	1	2	3
Does not really relate to anyone, even close family members	0	1	2	3
Only relates to one or two close family members	0	1	2	3
Does not show much affection	0	1	2	3
Does not readily learn appropriate behavior from role models	0	1	2	3
Often does not understand abstract social concepts such as "be kind"	0	1	2	3
Misunderstands other people's behavior or feelings	0	1	2	3

Difficulties with friendships

Seems to be unaware of the presence of others	0	1	2	3
Does not attempt to make friends with others	0	1	2	3
Tries but is unsuccessful in developing friendships with peers	0	1	2	3
Does not join in play activities, games, etc.	0	1	2	3
Is very wary of strangers	0	1	2	3
Is inhibited with strangers	0	1	2	3
Does not understand sharing	0	1	2	3
Does not understand turn taking	0	1	2	3

Difficulties understanding socially appropriate behavior

Says or does socially inappropriate things	0	1	2	3
Does not get embarrassed by social gaffes	0	1	2	3
Asks for explicit feedback such as "Am I giggling too much?"	0	1	2	3

Communication difficulties

Has no spoken language	0	1	2	3
Has a significant delay in spoken language	0	1	2	3
Uses language repetitively; repeats what other person has just said	0	1	2	3
Uses language repetitively; repeats himself or herself over and over	0	1	2	3
Uses odd, meaningless words or phrases repeatedly	0	1	2	3
Hears but does not respond appropriately when spoken to	0	1	2	3
Has significant difficulties with turn taking in conversation	0	1	2	3
Repeats same conversational pattern over and over	0	1	2	3
Has great difficulties understanding or using mime	0	1	2	3
Has great difficulties deliberately imitating speech or action	0	1	2	3
Does not play imaginatively	0	1	2	3
Takes things very literally	0	1	2	3

Unusual physical mannerisms

Engages in repetitive movements (e.g., hand clapping or body rocking)	0	1	2	3
Flickers own fingers close to face and watches them intently	0	1	2	3
Is poorly coordinated	0	1	2	3
Has a stiff or tiptoe walk, unusual arm movements when walking	0	1	2	3
Is very sensitive to some smells, textures, tastes	0	1	2	3
Has an unusually high threshold for pain or high/low temperatures	0	1	2	3
Causes self-injury, engages in biting, picking, head banging	0	1	2	3

Inflexible interests and adherence to routines

Has intense preoccupation with a specific object or topic (e.g., keys, fires, ambulances)	0	1	2	3
Is distressed by small changes in routine	0	1	2	3
Adheres to unnecessary, meaningless routines	0	1	2	3
Is preoccupied with parts of objects	0	1	2	3
Is fascinated by spinning or flickering items	0	1	2	3
Engages in repetitive activities such as lining up toys in certain order over and over	0	1	2	3

Exceptional "islands" of memory or skill

Has extraordinary memory for some specific information (e.g., train timetables)	0	1	2	3
Has exceptional technical skill (e.g., in music), but creative expression is lacking	0	1	2	3

Additional comments and observations:

AUTISM

Autism is one of a number of pervasive developmental disorders.
It can also be known as:

- Autism Spectrum Disorder
- Childhood Autism
- Kanner's Autism
- Early Infantile Autism

A pattern of difficulties that has many autistic features, but which does not meet all the diagnostic criteria for Autism may be called:

- Pervasive Developmental Disorder
- Atypical Autism

Characteristics of Autism

Autism is marked by a severe impairment in socialization and language. The condition can range from profound to mild. Students with mild Autism are sometimes referred to as "high functioning."

A student with Autism has significantly restricted communication skills. There may be no spoken language at all. Language may be present, but it may be disordered and unusual, including repetitive use of language (saying the same thing over and over again) or echolalia (repeating what another person has said). Turn taking in conversation is often significantly restricted.

Students with Autism may have unusual physical mannerisms such as rocking or hand flapping. Their general movements (walking, running, etc.) may be clumsy or poorly coordinated.

Students with Autism often have very inflexible interests and adherence to routines. For example, a student with Autism may accept only a very restricted range of foods. He or she may be inflexible about the way food is served, perhaps insisting on the same cup at every meal or that the food has to be cut or placed on the plate in a certain way.

Some students with Autism are fascinated by spinning or flickering objects or by a particular class of objects, for example, things that open and shut, vehicles with sirens, or anything with a switch.

Most students with Autism find change very difficult. They may become exceptionally distressed by small changes to routine or environment.

Students with Autism have marked problems in interpersonal relationships. Eye contact may be extremely limited, and they may find it very difficult to interact with peers or adults.

The majority of students with Autism also have Cognitive Disabilities, although there may be isolated "islands" of exceptional skill or talent, such as an extraordinary ability to remember dates or do complex mental arithmetic.

Because Autism is generally a serious disorder, it is often recognized during the preschool years. The infant's failure to develop normal socialization and early language skills combined with the early development of unusual behaviors will often prompt parents to seek advice during the child's first few years of life.

Causes of Autism

Autism is still not completely understood, although it is accepted that the condition is caused by an inherent dysfunction in brain activity. Autism is usually a congenital disorder, intrinsic to the student, although it can be associated with neurological impairments associated with encephalitis, Fragile X syndrome, and other medical conditions. It is not caused by adverse social or emotional circumstances as was once thought. Children with an autistic sibling have a higher than average risk of Autism.

Other Conditions With Characteristics Similar to Autism

Asperger Syndrome

Autism and Asperger Syndrome are both part of the Autism spectrum. A distinction between Asperger Syndrome and Autism can generally be made by reference to the severity of the condition and also by the development of the student's language skills. Autistic students have a marked impairment in their language, whereas students with Asperger Syndrome may have very well-developed language, but deficits in the nonverbal, perceptual reasoning area.

Language Impairment

Students with severe Language Impairment may also show some traits characteristic of Autism. A severe impairment in communication (caused by a Language Impairment and not Autism) may also be accompanied by poor socialization, resistance to change, and some obsessional behaviors.

Childhood Disintegrative Disorder and Rett's Disorder

These conditions are marked by normal development in the early months or years of life followed by deterioration in functioning, when autistic-like features begin to emerge after a period of normal development.

Disorders or Difficulties That May Accompany Autism

Autism is a complex disorder, which, in itself, has many facets. The student with Autism may have marked problems with concentration, may be poorly coordinated, may show strong signs of anxiety, and will almost inevitably have learning difficulties. Generally speaking, all of these difficulties come under the umbrella of the condition we know as Autism.

Autism and Mental Retardation (Cognitive Disability)

Mental Retardation is strongly associated with Autism. It is estimated that 75% of students with Autism also have a Cognitive Disability or Mental Retardation. The correct diagnosis can only be made after expert clinical assessment.

Professionals Who May Be Involved

Multidisciplinary Team

Autism is generally a complex, severe disorder, which, generally speaking, requires intensive, ongoing input from a multidisciplinary team.

Teachers

In the school setting, the student will, in most cases, have a high need for specialist input. In a general class, the student may need a teacher's aide to help interpret the teacher's instructions, modify tasks, and give the student support both academically and socially.

It is highly likely that the student with Autism will require intensive individual or small group support with a special educator. Obviously, this will vary according to the particular student's needs. A differentiated curriculum and individualized teaching will, in most cases, be essential.

Speech Therapists

Speech therapists may be involved in supporting the development of play and communication skills. This may include support for symbolic and imaginative play, training in the use of signing or communication devices, and of course, the development of oral communication (listening and responding).

Behavior Management Specialists

A psychiatrist, psychologist, or teacher with special expertise in behavior management may support teachers and parents in managing the student with Autism, with the goal of increasing socialization skills and decreasing the incidence and severity of inappropriate behaviors.

Pediatricians

A pediatrician will generally be involved to support the overall medical input for the student with Autism and to monitor general health functions.

Social Workers

A social worker may be involved to support parents, siblings, and peers of the student with Autism.

Action Plans for Children and Adolescents With Autism

- Ensure that a multidisciplinary team is set up, so that expertise from various professional fields can be brought together.
- It is often appropriate to appoint one person in the multidisciplinary team as the family's contact person. This means that all communication is filtered through that person, so that the family has one person to deal with, rather than several.
- Autism is a broad-based disorder, so very carefully consider not only academic, but also social and emotional needs.

- Most students with Autism have difficulties with shifts in routine or with unexpected events. Arrange the learning environment so that there is as much security, predictability, and consistency as possible.
- Introduce changes in staffing or physical location in small, incremental steps. Arrange early visits to a new classroom well before the student has to attend school in that classroom on a full-time basis.
- Talk to parents and caregivers to establish the student's particular idiosyncrasies with regard to things or events that may alarm, upset, or delight the student.
- Ensure that there is sufficient social support for the student, especially when the student is integrated with a group of peers, such as in a general classroom or schoolyard.
- At recreation times, it may be appropriate to set up a small play area where the student with Autism may play with other, invited children and where there is adult supervision, support, and facilitation.
- Ensure that the student's program includes as much life skills experience as possible. Becoming familiar with the outside environment, using public transportation, visiting public places, accessing community facilities, and being able to participate in normal community activities will be an important part of the student's overall personal development.
- If necessary, consider offering respite care to the family of the student with Autism, in recognition of the high demands that such a child may place on the family unit.

RECOMMENDED FURTHER READING

Reaching Out, Joining In: Teaching Social Skills to Young Children With Autism (Topics in Autism)
Authors: Mary Jane Weiss, Sandra L. Harris
Date of publication: 2001
Publisher: Woodbine House
ISBN: 1890627240

Educating Children with Autism
Author: National Research Council
Date of publication: 2001
Publisher: National Academy Press; 1st edition
ISBN: 0309072697

Behavioral Intervention for Young Children With Autism: A Manual for Parents and Professionals
Authors: Catherine Maurice, Gina Green, Stephen C. Luce
Date of publication: 1996
Publisher: Pro Ed
ISBN: 0890796831

Activity Schedules for Children With Autism: Teaching Independent Behavior (Topics in Autism)
Authors: Lynn E. McClannahan, Patricia J. Krantz
Date of publication: 2003
Publisher: Woodbine House
ISBN: 093314993X

Autism: A Practical Guide for Teachers and Parents
Author: Patricia Howlin
Date of publication: 1998
Publisher: John Wiley & Sons
ISBN: 0471976237

Relationship Development Intervention With Young Children: Social and Emotional Development Activities for Asperger Syndrome, Autism, PDD and NLD
Authors: Steven E. Gutstein, Rachelle K. Shelly
Date of publication: 2002
Publisher: Jessica Kingsley
ISBN: 1843107147

REFERENCES FOR AUTISM

Achenbach, T. M. (1991). *Manual for the child behavior checklist.* Burlington, VT: Department of Psychiatry, University of Vermont.

American Psychiatric Association. (1994). *Diagnostic and statistical manual of mental disorders* (4th ed.).Washington, DC: Author.

Cohen, D. J., & Volkmar, F. (Eds.). (1997). *Handbook of autism and pervasive developmental disorders.* New York: John Wiley & Sons.

Frith, U. (1989). *Autism: Explaining the enigma.* Oxford, UK: Basil Blackwell.

Lord, C., Rutter, M., & Le Couteur, A. (1994). Autism Diagnostic Interview–Revised: A revised version of a diagnostic interview for caregivers of individuals with possible pervasive developmental disorders. *Journal of Autism and Developmental Disorders, 24,* 659–685.

World Health Organization. (2000). *ICIDH-2: International classification of functioning, disability and health.* Geneva, Switzerland: Author.

THE ASPERGER SYNDROME CHECKLIST

Glynis Hannell, BA (Hons.), MSc Registered Psychologist

Student's name _____   Date _____   Student's age _____

Name of person completing checklist _____

Relationship to student _____

Each item that applies to the child or adolescent should be checked off using the following rating scale.

0 Not at all, does not apply
1 Mild, sometimes observed, applies to some extent
2 Moderate, often observed, certainly applies
3 Severe, frequently observed, strongly applies

*Please use **0** to indicate that an item has been considered and does not apply. If the **0** is not checked, it is not clear if the item has been overlooked.*

Poor social skills

Has few if any friends	0	1	2	3
Seems to find it difficult to read social situations	0	1	2	3
Makes inappropriate comments or does socially inappropriate things	0	1	2	3
Seems unaware of or disinterested in peer group pressure	0	1	2	3
Often chooses solitary activities	0	1	2	3
Does not initiate or join in games with other children	0	1	2	3
Tries to make friends but is socially clumsy	0	1	2	3
Does not seek to share interests with others	0	1	2	3
Does not understand the moral in stories or films	0	1	2	3

Inflexible

Becomes very unsettled if something unexpected happens	0	1	2	3
Needs a lot of preparation if routine has to be changed	0	1	2	3
Does not really enjoy new experiences	0	1	2	3
Is unwilling to try new foods, clothes, etc.	0	1	2	3
Does not enjoy surprises	0	1	2	3
Insists on sticking to routines that are unnecessary	0	1	2	3
Likes things in a certain order (e.g., toys in order of size)	0	1	2	3

Limited emotional understanding and unusual emotions

Seems to find it hard to understand how other people are feeling	0	1	2	3
Asks for explicit information about others' feelings (e.g., "Are you angry at me?")	0	1	2	3
Seems "flat" and expressionless when strong emotion is called for	0	1	2	3
Gets very emotional over small issues	0	1	2	3
Gets very anxious when this is not warranted	0	1	2	3

Egocentric

Can only see things from his or her own point of view	0	1	2	3
Expects others to read his or her mind	0	1	2	3

Difficulties with nonverbal communication

Has poor eye contact (too little or too much)	0	1	2	3
Poor judge of social distance (e.g., stands too close to others)	0	1	2	3
Is "wooden" when cuddled	0	1	2	3
Does not always understand facial expression or gesture	0	1	2	3
Finds it very difficult to mime or to mimic others	0	1	2	3

Restricted interests

Has an intense and prolonged interest in a topic (e.g., trains, electrical circuits)	0	1	2	3
Has a fascination for facts and figures (e.g., timetables, street directories, dates)	0	1	2	3
Has a preoccupation with parts of objects, how things work	0	1	2	3
Is obsessed by a particular book or computer game	0	1	2	3

Unusual language

Is very pedantic and "speaks like a professor"	0	1	2	3
Has an odd accent; people think he or she comes from overseas	0	1	2	3
Has unusual intonation (e.g., speaks in a loud monotone)	0	1	2	3
Often talks nonstop regardless of whether listener is interested or not	0	1	2	3
Uses idiosyncratic patterns of speech	0	1	2	3
Uses repetitive speech	0	1	2	3

Takes things very literally

Does not understand jokes, puns, or metaphors	0	1	2	3
Reads very accurately, but comprehension of what is read is poor	0	1	2	3

Poor coordination or unusual sensory awareness

Is physically clumsy	0	1	2	3
Has poor handwriting, immature drawing, and untidy bookwork	0	1	2	3
Is unusually sensitive to textures of clothes or food	0	1	2	3
Is unusually sensitive to smells	0	1	2	3

Unusual physical mannerisms

Flaps or twirls hands	0	1	2	3
Has an unusual gait, may have stiff legs or exaggerated arm movements	0	1	2	3
Likes to run in a set pattern (e.g., in circles or on a particular route)	0	1	2	3
Runs on the spot or twirls, especially when agitated	0	1	2	3

Additional comments and observations:

ASPERGER SYNDROME

Asperger Syndrome is also known as:

- Autism Spectrum Disorder
- Nonverbal Learning Disorder (not all professionals agree with this categorization)
- Semantic Pragmatic Disorder (not all professionals agree with this categorization)

Characteristics of Asperger Syndrome

Children and adolescents with Asperger Syndrome might not be diagnosed until they are well into their school years. Their difficulties may be subtle, or they may be quite obvious.

Asperger Syndrome is characterized by difficulties with socialization, a tendency to be uncomfortable with change in routine, and obsessional interests in a specific area such as maps, timetables, or electrical circuits. The obsessional behavior may also encompass an obsessional interest in one particular book, film, or television show.

Socialization difficulties are evident in the way in which the student fails to "read" nonverbal or implicit messages. The student with Asperger Syndrome may often speak well and at length but be poor at maintaining his or her part in a dialogue.

Causes of Asperger Syndrome

There is a genetic link in Asperger Syndrome, with family members sometimes showing similar characteristics. It is caused by an irregularity in brain function.

Other Conditions With Characteristics Similar to Asperger Syndrome

Autism

Autism and Asperger Syndrome are both in the Autism spectrum. However, Asperger Syndrome is characterized by adequate, and sometimes even excellent, language skills and milder, more subtle socialization difficulties than might be observed in a student with Autism.

Language Impairment

Students with Language Impairment can also show characteristics of Asperger Syndrome, particularly in the difficulties they experience in communication and socialization. Some students with severe Language Impairment may show some obsessional behaviors. Expert assessment is required to make this differential diagnosis.

Anxiety Disorder

Students with Anxiety Disorders may have obsessional behaviors such as repetitive hand washing.

Disorders or Difficulties That May Accompany Asperger Syndrome

Asperger Syndrome and Giftedness

Some students with Asperger Syndrome are also intellectually gifted. It can be clinically difficult to distinguish between the in-depth interest in a topic shown by an intellectually gifted student and the obsessional interest shown by a student with Asperger Syndrome.

Asperger Syndrome and Anxiety

Many students with Asperger Syndrome also have Anxiety Disorders. A student with Asperger Syndrome is inflexible and finds change difficult. He or she may readily become very anxious about minor changes that would not worry another student at all, such as the prospect of a school camp, the presence of a relief teacher, or change in the way in which the classroom or school timetable is arranged.

Asperger Syndrome and Attention-Deficit Disorder

Many students with Asperger Syndrome also have Attention-Deficit Disorder.

Asperger Syndrome and Developmental Coordination Disorder

Students with Asperger Syndrome quite frequently have problems with perceptual reasoning. This may be associated with Developmental Coordination Disorders or Dyspraxia. This may mean that the student with Asperger Syndrome can talk quite well but fails to present written work or graphics to the same standard.

Asperger Syndrome and Oppositional Defiant Disorder

The characteristics of Asperger Syndrome (inflexible, difficulties with interpersonal relationships) will readily contribute to behavioral problems. The student with Asperger Syndrome may often appear oppositional or defiant because of communication problems or inflexibility. This is likely to be much more marked if adults working with the student do not recognize that the student has Asperger Syndrome and fail to adapt teaching and behavior management strategies accordingly.

Asperger Syndrome and Depression

Students with Asperger Syndrome can readily become depressed, particularly as they are likely to experience ongoing difficulties with socialization. The student with Asperger Syndrome may lack the skills to establish stable, positive relationships with peers and can easily become the victim of teasing and harassment.

Professionals Who May Be Involved

Teachers

Most students with Asperger Syndrome will be in the general class, with appropriate support on the basis of their individual needs, so that classroom teachers will have primary responsibility for the student's day-to-day support and management. Special educators may work with associated learning difficulties and may be part of the team that supports the student with socialization.

Behavior Management Specialists

Specialist support from a psychologist, psychiatrist, or behavior management specialist may be needed to assist the student with anxiety, obsessional behavior, and socialization skills.

Action Plans for Students With Asperger Syndrome

- The classroom teacher and special needs teacher will need to work together with parents to establish an understanding of the student's particular, idiosyncratic needs. For instance, some students with Asperger Syndrome may be hypersensitive to loud noises or find some physical sensations highly distressing. These idiosyncrasies need to be well understood to avoid unnecessary distress.
- Students with Asperger Syndrome are more comfortable when there is continuity, predictability, and security. They are much less comfortable in open-ended or unpredictable situations. Their classroom environment therefore needs to be one that has a steady, explicit routine.
- The student with Asperger Syndrome will need good preparation when the inevitable transitions in life occur. For instance, changing from one grade level to another, working with a new teacher, or changing classrooms will all need to be handled sensitively so that the student has time to acclimatize.
- Sarcasm, satire, and jokes are taken literally, and this can cause great distress. Teachers therefore need to be very sensitive to how the student perceives what is said. Clear, factual statements are the most easily understood.
- The student may often need adults to interpret some events for them. For instance, when a joke has been made, the student with Asperger Syndrome will benefit if adults can explain that it was a joke, and why it was funny.
- Students with Asperger Syndrome often need explicit social skills teaching. Other children may intuitively understand appropriate social distance, how to make friends, or how to respond to a visitor. The student with Asperger Syndrome may need to be taught these things explicitly and to be given guided practice and coaching in real-life situations.

- The student may need to be taught how to interpret emotion. For instance, instead of just being able to judge that a teacher is getting angry with them by the teacher's body language and tone of voice, the student with Asperger Syndrome may need to be told "I am very angry about this."
- The student may need explicit teaching about nonverbal communication to help him or her to interpret facial expression, tone of voice, and other nonverbal behaviors.
- Many students with Asperger Syndrome have excellent oral language but poor fine motor and perceptual skills. They may need additional teaching or adjustments and accommodations to take account of their problems with neatness, coordination, bookwork, and so forth.

RECOMMENDED FURTHER READING

The Explosive Child: A New Approach for Understanding and Parenting Easily Frustrated, Chronically Inflexible Children
Author: Ross W. Greene
Date of publication: 2001
Publisher: HarperCollins
ISBN: 0060931027

Asperger's Syndrome: A Guide for Parents and Professionals
Authors: Tony Attwood, Lorna Wing
Date of publication: 1998
Publisher: Jessica Kingsley
ISBN: 1853025771

Hitchhiking Through Asperger Syndrome
Authors: Lise Pyles, Tony Attwood
Date of publication: 2001
Publisher: Jessica Kingsley
ISBN: 1853029378

Asperger Syndrome and Your Child: A Parent's Guide
Authors: Michael D. Powers, Janet Poland
Date of publication: 2002
Publisher: Harper Resource
ISBN: 0066209439

REFERENCES FOR ASPERGER SYNDROME

Achenbach, T. M. (1991). *Manual for the child behavior checklist.* Burlington, VT: Department of Psychiatry, University of Vermont.
American Psychiatric Association. (1994). *Diagnostic and statistical manual of mental disorders* (4th ed.).Washington, DC.

Attwood, T. (2001). *Asperger's syndrome: A guide for parents and professionals.* London: Jessica Kinglsey.

Cohen, D. J., & Volkmar, F. (Eds.). (1997). *Handbook of autism and pervasive developmental disorders.* New York: John Wiley & Sons.

Frith, U. (1989). *Autism: Explaining the enigma.* Oxford, UK: Basil Blackwell.

Frith, U. (Ed.). (1991). *Autism and Asperger's syndrome.* Cambridge, UK: Cambridge University Press.

Schepler, E., Mesibov, G., & Kunce, L. (Eds.). (1998). *Asperger syndrome and high functioning autism.* New York: Plenum Press.

Wolff, S. (1991). Asperger's syndrome. *Archives of Diseases in Childhood, 66,* 178–179.

Wolff, S. (1995). *Loners: The life path of unusual children.* London: Routledge.

World Health Organization. (2000). *ICIDH-2: International classification of functioning, disability and health.* Geneva, Switzerland: Author.

EMOTIONAL OR BEHAVIORAL DISORDERS AND EMOTIONAL DISTURBANCE

Five checklists are included in this section:

- Anxiety Disorder
- Selective Mutism
- Depression
- Conduct Disorder
- Oppositional Defiant Disorder

DEFINITION OF EMOTIONAL DISTURBANCE: INDIVIDUALS WITH DISABILITIES EDUCATION ACT (IDEA)

IDEA defines Emotional Disturbance as follows:

The term means a condition exhibiting one or more of the following characteristics over a long period of time and to a marked degree that adversely affects a child's educational performance:

(A) An inability to learn that cannot be explained by intellectual, sensory, or health factors.

(B) An inability to build or maintain satisfactory interpersonal relationships with peers and teachers.

(C) Inappropriate types of behavior or feelings under normal circumstances.

(D) A general pervasive mood of unhappiness or depression.

(E) A tendency to develop physical symptoms or fears associated with personal or school problems.

The term includes schizophrenia. The term does not apply to children who are socially maladjusted, unless it is determined that they have an emotional disturbance.

HOW TO USE THE CHECKLISTS

Complete the Checklist

Fill in the administrative details at the top of the form.

Consider each item in turn. Record your subjective evaluation of the extent to which that item applies to the student.

Add any additional comments or qualifications in the space provided at the end of the questionnaire.

Interpret the Checklist

The checklist is a screening instrument, and the ratings that you have selected reflect your observations of the child or adolescent. The more items that apply to a child or adolescent, and the more frequently these items have been observed, the more likely it is that the child or adolescent has an Emotional or Behavioral Disturbance. However, it is important to remember that several other conditions have similar characteristics and that specialist assessment is necessary for formal diagnosis.

For your information, descriptions of the disorders, similar conditions, and conditions that may accompany each disorder are provided.

Decide Whether to Refer for Further Assessment

The checklists will help you to decide whether to refer the student for further assessment. Guidelines are given on pages 5 and 7 for interpreting the rating scales.

Look at the Subcategories of the Checklist

The subcategories will help you isolate any specific areas of difficulty and plan appropriate intervention strategies targeted to the student's individual needs. The action plans that follow will help give you some practical ideas on intervention strategies.

THE ANXIETY DISORDER CHECKLIST

Glynis Hannell, BA (Hons.), MSc Registered Psychologist

Student's name _____ Date _____ Student's age _____

Name of person completing checklist _____

Relationship to student _____

Each item that applies to the child or adolescent should be checked off using the following rating scale.

0 Not at all, does not apply
1 Mild, sometimes observed, applies to some extent
2 Moderate, often observed, certainly applies
3 Severe, frequently observed, strongly applies

*Please use **0** to indicate that an item has been considered and does not apply. If the **0** is not checked, it is not clear if the item has been overlooked.*

Disturbed sleep

Has difficulties getting to sleep, scared of the dark, hears noises, etc.	0	1	2	3
Is afraid of being alone at night	0	1	2	3
Has nightmares or night terrors	0	1	2	3

Afraid of new experiences

Wants to do something new but panics at the last minute and will not go	0	1	2	3
Worries excessively before a new experience	0	1	2	3
Refuses to try new things because of anxiety	0	1	2	3
Panics when a new experience is forced on him or her	0	1	2	3
Gets extremely anxious before the start of a new school week, term, or year	0	1	2	3
Needs a lot of preparation before being able to cope with new experience	0	1	2	3
Hides or locks self away to avoid anxiety-provoking situations	0	1	2	3

Has physical signs of anxiety

Has nervous blink, twitch, or other mannerism	0	1	2	3
Feels numb or complains of tingling sensations	0	1	2	3
Gets sweaty palms when anxious	0	1	2	3

Goes pale under pressure	0	1	2	3
Vomits (or feels nauseous) in stressful situations	0	1	2	3
Has breathing difficulties or choking sensation when anxious	0	1	2	3
Has panic attacks and becomes visibly overwhelmed by anxiety	0	1	2	3
Complains of increased or irregular heart rate	0	1	2	3
Has a tantrum or clings when frightened or anxious	0	1	2	3
"Freezes" and will not move or speak when anxious	0	1	2	3
Is afraid of dying, going crazy, or losing control	0	1	2	3

Anxious about being separated from parent

Resists being separated from parent (e.g., at start of school day)	0	1	2	3
Worries about parents' well-being when separated from them	0	1	2	3
Is reluctant to sleep without parent being near	0	1	2	3
Is reluctant to stay away from home overnight	0	1	2	3
Worries about how long it will be before parent returns to pick him or her up	0	1	2	3
Panics if parent is not there at the appointed time	0	1	2	3

Specific phobias

Has extreme fear of animals (a particular animal or insect, or animals in general)	0	1	2	3
Is frightened by clowns or other "entertaining" characters	0	1	2	3
Cannot watch cartoons suitable for age group without being frightened	0	1	2	3
Is overanxious about medical or dental procedures, refuses treatment, panics	0	1	2	3
Is very fearful about going into some places	0	1	2	3
Is excessively anxious about everyday risks (e.g., storms, thunder, water)	0	1	2	3
Is very uncomfortable in enclosed or crowded spaces	0	1	2	3
Has excessive anxiety about germs, accidents, death, and illness	0	1	2	3

Obsessions or compulsions

Attempts to prevent a dreaded event by obsessional behavior	0	1	2	3
Is distressed by thoughts, images, or impulses that will not go away	0	1	2	3

Unusually upset by tragic events

Is made extremely anxious by news items about disasters, terrorism attacks, etc.	0	1	2	3
Plans elaborate escape or protection strategies to avoid possible traumas	0	1	2	3

Talks excessively about catastrophes that have occurred or might occur	0	1	2	3
Continually asks for reassurance about possible catastrophes	0	1	2	3
Has a prolonged and severe reaction to a trauma he or she has experienced	0	1	2	3

Social anxiety

Is excessively shy with unfamiliar people	0	1	2	3
Is unusually reluctant to participate in group activities appropriate to age	0	1	2	3
Is very sensitive and self-conscious, very easily humiliated or embarrassed	0	1	2	3
Dislikes being watched, even in everyday activities such as eating or playing	0	1	2	3
Is very shy and reluctant to perform, even in a group	0	1	2	3

Family history

Other family members have (or have had) an Anxiety Disorder	Yes	No	Don't know

Additional comments and observations:

ANXIETY DISORDER

Characteristics of Anxiety Disorder

Anxiety can take various forms and can include panic attacks, Obsessive-Compulsive Disorder, and specific phobias.

All anxiety conditions are marked by feelings of fearfulness and apprehension. Often, physical symptoms, such as shortness of breath, racing heart, and feelings of choking or losing control, accompany the subjective feeling of anxiety.

Some students may show obsessive/compulsive symptoms as a characteristic of their Anxiety Disorder. They may persistently repeat actions such as washing their hands; need to count in a particular, ritualistic way; or insist on special routines.

Some students may have a specific phobia; for instance, they may have a school phobia, in which thinking about going to school and actually approaching school induce a panic reaction. This may also involve vomiting or hysterical behavior such as locking themselves in the bathroom or refusing to get out of the car. The student may agree that he or she will be able to go to school the next day, but once the event is imminent, the anxiety intensifies and he or she panics.

Some students, particularly younger children, may have specific phobias such as fear of storms, clowns, or particular places.

Students who are prone to anxiety may also become extremely anxious about natural or world events; for example, they may worry excessively that an earthquake will occur in their home locality.

Causes of Anxiety Disorder

Students with anxiety are more likely than others to have a family history of Anxiety Disorder.

Anxiety is a normal human emotion that has an important and positive function in guiding children in their behavior. Anxiety about the consequences usually stops children from taking undue risks or engaging in dangerous activities. However, an excess of anxiety can be detrimental, in that it makes the student unnecessarily fearful about everyday experiences.

There is a natural variation among children with regard to their intrinsic tendency to become anxious in some situations. This tendency can be exacerbated by inappropriate treatment by adults. Harsh treatment of fearful behavior can increase anxiety levels, as the student becomes afraid of becoming anxious and then there are two underlying emotions (the fear itself and the fear of the adult's reaction to this fear). On the other hand, undue collusion with the child's fears can extend the duration, frequency, or intensity of the anxiety reaction. For example, a child who is fearful of water and is never allowed near water will find it hard to overcome that fear.

Anxious children are often perfectionists. This means that they have significant anxiety that they are not going to be good enough. They may be excessively concerned about criticism or failure, and they need a high level of approval.

Other Conditions With Characteristics Similar to Anxiety Disorder

Asperger Syndrome

Students with Asperger Syndrome are often obsessional and inflexible. They can become agitated and distressed if things do not follow the expected pattern.

Child Abuse

Students who have been abused may appear to be overly fearful if the abuse is not known to adults making the judgment. Once the situation is known, the student's anxiety may be seen to be quite valid.

Disorders or Difficulties That May Accompany Anxiety Disorder

Anxiety Disorder and Selective Mutism

Selective Mutism is a very specific form of Anxiety Disorder. (See the Selective Mutism checklist on page 47.)

Anxiety Disorder and Obsessive-Compulsive Disorder

Obsessive and compulsive behaviors are symptoms and components of Anxiety Disorder.

Anxiety Disorder and Asperger Syndrome

Although the characteristics of Asperger Syndrome and Anxiety Disorder are similar, it is quite common for both conditions to occur concurrently. Many students with Asperger Syndrome have a marked Anxiety Disorder with regard to specific events or life in general.

Professionals Who May Be Involved

Teachers

Class teachers and student counselors will in all probability work as a team with the student's parents to support the student with regard to his or her anxieties.

Psychologists, Psychiatrists, and Counselors

A psychologist, student counselor, or psychiatrist may also be involved in managing the anxiety symptoms. Medication may be indicated, if the anxiety is severe or prolonged.

Action Plans for the Student With Anxiety Disorder

- Treating Anxiety Disorder often requires the expertise of a specialist in the treatment of anxiety.

- The standard treatment procedure is cognitive behavior therapy. This means that the therapist working with the anxious student helps the student move away from an emotional response toward a response that involves cognition and logic. This helps the student make a realistic appraisal of the situation, which in turn helps constrain the emotional response.

- It is appropriate for adults to protect children from some types of information, if it is felt that the information may cause excessive anxiety.

- Anxious students are more comfortable where they are in a predictable, secure, and nurturing environment.

- Anxiety usually increases if well-meaning adults try to force the issue, so if possible, avoid forcing the anxious student into a situation in which he or she may panic. For instance, a child who is fearful of water may be traumatized if forcibly immersed in water, and his or her fearfulness may well increase.

- The best way to manage Anxiety Disorder is to try to stabilize the student and then gradually build his or her resilience with regard to the trigger for anxiety. Professional therapists may use special techniques such as visualization and relaxation training. The parent or classroom teacher can help by providing relaxed, playful opportunities to be near and around whatever it is that triggers anxiety (without excessive pressure).

- If a student does have a panic attack, it is important for adults to remain calm, speak quietly, and ensure that the student feels secure. It is important to remember that the student's reactions at this stage are driven by emotion, not logic, and so uncomplicated reassurances usually work best.

RECOMMENDED FURTHER READING

Worried No More: Help and Hope for Anxious Children
Author: Aureen Pinto Wagner
Date of publication: 2002
Publisher: Lighthouse Press
ISBN: 0967734734

School Phobia, Panic Attacks and Anxiety in Children
Author: Márianna Csóti
Date of publication: 2003
Publisher: J. Kingsley
ISBN: 1843100916

Your Anxious Child: How Parents and Teachers Can Relieve Anxiety in Children
Author: John S. Dacey, Lisa B. Fiore
Date of publication: 2001
Publisher: Jossey-Bass; 1st edition
ISBN: 0787960403

**Up and Down the Worry Hill: A Children's Book About
Obsessive-Compulsive Disorder and Its Treatment**
Author: Aureen Pinto Wagner, Paul A. Jutton (illustrator)
Date of publication: 2000
Publisher: Lighthouse Press
ISBN: 0967734703

The Anxiety Cure for Kids: A Guide for Parents
Authors: Elizabeth DuPont Spencer, Robert L. DuPont, Caroline M. DuPont
Date of publication: 2003
Publisher: John Wiley & Sons
ISBN: 0471263613

Keys to Parenting Your Anxious Child (Barron's Parenting Keys)
Author: Katharina Manassis
Date of publication: 1996
Publisher: Barron's Educational Series
ISBN: 0812096053

REFERENCES FOR ANXIETY DISORDER

Achenbach, T. M. (1991). *Manual for the child behavior checklist.* Burlington, VT: Department of Psychiatry, University of Vermont.
American Psychiatric Association. (1994). *Diagnostic and statistical manual of mental disorders* (4th ed.). Washington, DC: Author.
Angold, A., & Costello, E. J. (2000). The Child and Adolescent Psychiatric Assessment (CAPA). *Journal of the American Academy of Child and Adolescent Psychiatry, 39,* 39–48.
Beidel, D. C., & Morris, T. L. (1995). Social phobia. In C. March (Ed.), *Anxiety disorders in children and adolescents* (pp. 181–211). New York: Guilford Press.
Cichetti, D., & Cohen, D. J. (Eds.). (1995). *Developmental psychopathology: Risk, disorder and adaptation.* New York: John Wiley & Sons.
Eisen, A. R., Kearney, C. A., & Schaefer, C. E. (Eds.). (1995). *Clinical handbook of anxiety disorders in children and adolescents.* Northvale, NJ: Jason Aronson.
Harris, J., Tyre, C., & Wilkinson, C. (1993). Using the Child Behavior Checklist in ordinary primary schools. *British Journal of Educational Psychology, 63,* 245–260.
Hoge, R. D., & Andrews, D. A. (1992). Assessing conduct problems in the classroom. *Clinical Psychology Review, 12,* 1–20.
Ollendicak, N. J., King, T., & Yule, W. (Eds.). *International handbook of phobic and anxiety disorders in children & adolescents.* New York: Plenum Press.
Rapee, R. M., Barrett, P., Dadds, M. R., & Evans, L. (1994). Reliability of the *DMS-III-R* childhood anxiety disorders using structured interview: Inter-rater and parent-child agreement. *Journal of the American Academy of Child and Adolescent Psychiatry, 33,* 984–992.
Rutter, M., Taylor, E., & Hersov, L. (Eds.). (1994) . *Child and adolescent psychiatry: Modern approaches.* Cambridge, MA: Blackwell Science.
Silverman, W. K., & Nelles, W. B. (1998). The Anxiety Disorders Interview Schedule for Children. *Journal of the American Academy of Child and Adolescent Psychiatry, 27,* 772–778.

Sparrow, S. S., Balla, D. A., & Cicchetti, D. V. (2000). *Comprehensive psychological and psychoeducational assessment of children and adolescents: A developmental approach.* Boston: Allyn & Bacon.

Stroff, D. M., Breiling, J., & Maser, J. D. (Eds.). (1997). *Handbook of antisocial behavior.* New York: John Wiley & Sons.

Vasey, M. W. (1995). Social anxiety disorders. In A. R. Eisen, C. A. Kearney, & C. E. Schaefer (Eds.), *Clinical handbook of anxiety disorders in children and adolescents* (pp. 131–168). Washington, DC: Jason Aronson.

Walker, H. M. (1995). *The acting out child. Coping with classroom disruption* (2nd ed.). Boston: Allyn & Bacon.

World Health Organization. (1993). *The ICD-10 classification of mental and behavioral disorders: Diagnostic criteria research.* Geneva, Switzerland: Author.

World Health Organization. (2000). *ICIDH-2: International classification of functioning, disability and health.* Geneva, Switzerland: Author.

THE SELECTIVE MUTISM CHECKLIST

Glynis Hannell, BA (Hons.), MSc Registered Psychologist

Student's name _____ Date _____ Student's age _____

Name of person completing checklist _____

Relationship to student _____

Each item that applies to the child or adolescent should be checked off using the following rating scale.

0 Not at all, does not apply
1 Mild, sometimes observed, applies to some extent
2 Moderate, often observed, certainly applies
3 Severe, frequently observed, strongly applies

*Please use **0** to indicate that an item has been considered and does not apply. If the **0** is not checked, it is not clear if the item has been overlooked.*

Unwillingness to speak

Is reluctant to speak to anyone outside of family home	0	1	2	3
Is reluctant to speak to visitors to the family home	0	1	2	3
Is willing to speak to some family members but not others	0	1	2	3
May speak to children but not adults outside of the home	0	1	2	3
Is unwilling to speak to familiar people when observed by a stranger	0	1	2	3
Shows unwillingness to speak in first language (if multilingual)	0	1	2	3

Adequate language development

Does communicate adequately with familiar people	0	1	2	3

Subtle language difficulties

Was later than average in learning to talk	0	1	2	3
Has subtle language difficulties that are not easily recognized	0	1	2	3

Use of nonverbal communication

Uses gesture to communicate	0	1	2	3
Nods or shakes head appropriately when spoken to	0	1	2	3
Uses physical communication (e.g., leads adult by the hand to indicate needs)	0	1	2	3

Uses short, monotone grunts in place of words	0	1	2	3
Joins in group singing, but may stop if watched	0	1	2	3
May stare blankly when spoken to	0	1	2	3
May avoid eye contact	0	1	2	3

Problem lasts for more than a month

Has been unwilling to speak to some people for at least a month	0	1	2	3
Has been unwilling to speak in some settings for at least a month	0	1	2	3

Problem does not respond to pressure

Cannot be bribed into speaking	0	1	2	3
Does not respond to threats or punishments	0	1	2	3

There are no other reasons for unwillingness to speak

Is emotionally disturbed	Yes	No	Don't know
Has been traumatized	Yes	No	Don't know
Is autistic	Yes	No	Don't know
Has Cognitive Disability or Mental Retardation	Yes	No	Don't know
Has a receptive or expressive language disorder	Yes	No	Don't know
Is seriously ill	Yes	No	Don't know

Has had appropriate opportunity to speak

Speaks the same language as others	Yes	No	Don't know
Can hear adequately	Yes	No	Don't know
Has had normal socialization	Yes	No	Don't know

Cautious personality

Is chronically shy	0	1	2	3
Does not like to take risks of any kind	0	1	2	3
Is slow to gain confidence in new situations	0	1	2	3

Inflexibility

Is often stubborn over small matters	0	1	2	3
Was slow or resistant to toilet training	0	1	2	3
Is very picky about food, clothes, etc.	0	1	2	3
Often has tantrums if unable to get his or her own way	0	1	2	3
Can be rigid about routines	0	1	2	3
Does not like change	0	1	2	3
Can sometimes be obsessional, excessively neat, or fussy	0	1	2	3
Does not like unusual textures, tastes, or physical sensations	0	1	2	3

Family history

Other family members may have been similar in childhood	Yes	No	Don't know
Family history of language disorder	Yes	No	Don't know
At least one parent is quiet and reclusive	Yes	No	Don't know

Additional comments and observations:

SELECTIVE MUTISM

Characteristics of Selective Mutism

Selective Mutism describes a condition in which the child remains silent in some specific situations but is able to communicate within normal limits in others. Typically, the child may be verbally communicative at home but fail to speak at all in a setting such as at child care, in the classroom, or in a similar environment.

Children with Selective Mutism may communicate nonverbally by using facial expression, gestures, or physical expression, such as taking people by the hand to lead them to something of interest. Sometimes the child verbalizes but uses a different voice from normal or simply uses short grunts or monosyllables.

Usually the condition only lasts a few months, but it can be protracted in some cases.

Generally speaking, children with selective mutism are very resistant to deliberate attempts to make them speak. Indeed, trying to enforce speaking often is counterproductive and has the reverse effect.

Some children with Selective Mutism will speak at school, but only to peers, when they feel that they are not observed by adults.

Children who display Selective Mutism are usually relatively young. The condition may appear at preschool level, for instance, when the child attends child care or kindergarten, and may continue through the early years of schooling. It is very unusual for a child older than 8 or 9 years of age to display Selective Mutism.

Causes of Selective Mutism

There is no known cause of Selective Mutism, other than it generally occurs in children who are by nature shy or anxious. There may be a family history of Anxiety Disorders.

Other Conditions With Similar Characteristics to Selective Mutism

Language Impairment

Some children with a Language Impairment are very uncomfortable about using language, particularly in unfamiliar surroundings. They may experience difficulty and frustration in verbal communication, and so they withdraw unless they are feeling secure.

Speech Disorder

Similarly, children who have an articulation or speech difficulty may choose not to speak in situations in which they are not certain of being understood.

Multilingual Children

Children who speak more than one language may be uncomfortable at using a second language with which they are less confident. This might mean they speak freely in their first language in their home environment but are reluctant to communicate outside of the home using a second language.

Autism

Students with Autism are likely to have significantly impaired communication skills. However, they are clearly differentiated from students with Selective Mutism by the fact that their lack of communication is not selective and generally occurs across all environments.

Mental Retardation (Cognitive Disability)

Students with Mental Retardation may have impaired communication. They may be less verbal in situations in which they feel less secure or in which the communication environment is too complex for them to process.

Anxiety Disorder

An Anxiety Disorder is strongly associated with Selective Mutism, and it is often the case that a child may have both conditions concurrently.

Child Abuse

Children who are abused may become noncommunicative, particularly when they are deeply distressed.

Disorders or Difficulties That May Accompany Selective Mutism

Selective Mutism and Anxiety Disorder

The primary disorder that accompanies Selective Mutism is Anxiety Disorder. Typically, children with Selective Mutism are socially reserved or anxious and may have obsessive behaviors.

Selective Mutism and Language Impairment

Some students with Selective Mutism may have a subtle Language Impairment, which undermines their confidence in their own skills in verbal communication.

Selective Mutism and Oppositional Defiant Disorder

Some children who are unwilling to speak outside of the home environment are oppositional or defiant within it. The underlying characteristic seems to be that of control. Outside of the home environment, the child exerts control by refusing to speak; within the home, he or she seeks to control by being verbally defiant.

Professionals Who May Be Involved

Teachers

Teachers and special educators will have a role in supporting the child with Selective Mutism.

Speech Pathologists

A speech pathologist's services will be important in supporting the student's communication skills. It will also be important to establish that the child does in fact have normal receptive and expressive language, and that there is no Language Impairment underlying the child's reluctance to speak in some settings.

Psychiatrists or Psychologists

A psychiatrist or psychologist may be involved when Selective Mutism is severe or continues for an extended period of time. Medication can sometimes assist in treating the underlying anxiety.

Action Plans for Selective Mutism

- Selective Mutism is driven by anxiety and, sometimes, by oppositional behavior. Trying to force a child to speak generally has the opposite effect.
- Selective Mutism will be at its worst when adults demand that the child speaks, if there are rewards or punishments contingent on speaking, if the child is singled out to speak, and if there is an audience.
- Selective Mutism will be minimized in situations in which the child is free to choose to speak or not.
- Children are more comfortable about speaking if they do not have to make eye contact or speak to an obvious audience.
- It also helps if children can speak as softly or briefly as they like and if the fact that they are speaking is accepted without fuss or comment.
- Establish a secure and predictable routine in the preschool or school setting.
- Encourage the child to join in both physically and verbally, but do not force the issue.
- Talk to the child often, but without demanding a response.
- Children will generally speak first to an adult with whom they have developed a warm, positive rapport. Provide opportunities for the child to have a consistent caregiver and allow opportunities for child and caregiver to be together, without an audience. This is the most likely situation for the child to begin to speak to an adult outside of the home.
- Many children with Selective Mutism will speak to children, provided adults are out of hearing. Ensure that there are ample opportunities for

the child with Selective Mutism to play with peers, in situations where they are apparently unobserved and not overheard.

- If the child does talk to peers but not adults, it is sometimes possible to break down the child-adult communication barrier by a trusted, familiar adult joining in with the children's group and engaging in their play. For instance, a small group of children, including the child with Selective Mutism, are sitting at a table drawing and coloring. The adult sits beside the child (making no eye contact) and joins the activity and general chatter: "I'm doing mine blue. . . . Julia, can I please have the red? . . . I think I'll do another one. . . . Is that your brother?" First, only ask the child with Selective Mutism for physical responses, such as passing you a crayon that you need. Then ask a question that can quite naturally be given a nonverbal answer, such as nodding. Only then create openings for verbal answers. If the child still does not speak, do not force the issue. With time and patience, the barrier does usually come down.
- Encourage the child to communicate in any way that feels comfortable. For instance, encourage gesture, signing, the use of a communication board, or any other means of interaction.
- If possible, create a good bridge between home and school. A teacher or caregiver may visit the child at home, talking to the child's parents in a relaxed setting. The child may or may not participate verbally, but will often begin to warm to the adult, who is someone usually seen only in a school setting.
- Some children with Selective Mutism really want to participate verbally in their class, but do not have the courage to do so. They might sometimes prepare a video or an audiotape at home, which can be played to a teacher or to a small group of supportive peers as their means of contributing to the verbal exchange of the classroom.
- Some children with Selective Mutism will sing, count, read out loud, or speak through a puppet even though they will not speak spontaneously. These are all useful transition activities, helping break down the barriers of anxiety and reluctance to communicate.

RECOMMENDED FURTHER READING

Selective Mutism in Children
Authors: Sylvia Baldwin, Tony Cline
Date of publication: 2004
Publisher: Whurr
ISBN: 1861563620, all editions

Refusal to Speak: Treatment of Selective Mutism in Children (Child Therapy Series)
Authors: Sheila Spasaro, Charles E. Schaefer
Date of publication: 1999
Publisher: Jason Aronson
ISBN: 0765701251

REFERENCES FOR SELECTIVE MUTISM

American Psychiatric Association. (1994). *Diagnostic and statistical manual of mental disorders* (4th ed.).Washington, DC: Author.

Cantwell, D. P., & Baker, L. (1991). *Psychiatric and developmental disorders in children with communication disorder.* Washington, DC: American Psychiatric Press.

Eisen, A. R., Kearney, C. A., & Schaefer, C. E. (Eds.). (1995). *Clinical handbook of anxiety disorders in children and adolescents.* Northvale, NJ: Jason Aronson.

Leitenberg, H. (Ed.). (1991). *Handbook of social and evaluation anxiety.* New York: Plenum.

Thomas, A., & Chess, S. (1977). *Temperament and development.* New York: Brunner/Mazel.

Thomas, A., Chess, S., & Korn, S. J. (1982). The reality of difficult temperament. *Merrill Palmer Quarterly, 28,* 1–20.

Thomson, R. A. (1997). Sensitivity and security: New questions to ponder. *Child Development, 68,* 595–597.

THE CHILD AND ADOLESCENT DEPRESSION CHECKLIST

Glynis Hannell, BA (Hons.), MSc Registered Psychologist

Student's name _____ Date _____ Student's age _____

Name of person completing checklist _____

Relationship to student _____

Each item that applies to the child or adolescent should be checked off using the following rating scale.

0 Not at all, does not apply
1 Mild, sometimes observed, applies to some extent
2 Moderate, often observed, certainly applies
3 Severe, frequently observed, strongly applies

*Please use **0** to indicate that an item has been considered and does not apply. If the **0** is not checked, it is not clear if the item has been overlooked.*

Negative mood

Is negative about most things	0	1	2	3
Complains of being "fed up"	0	1	2	3
Complains of being bored	0	1	2	3
Often seems sad	0	1	2	3
Often seems flat and emotionless	0	1	2	3
Often seems angry and bad tempered	0	1	2	3
Cries easily	0	1	2	3
Irritable and touchy	0	1	2	3

Loss of interest and enjoyment

Has lost interest in things that used to be enjoyed	0	1	2	3
Not interested if suitable activities are suggested	0	1	2	3
Has lost sense of humor	0	1	2	3
Seems lazy and disinterested in most things	0	1	2	3
Does not seem to care about success in schoolwork, sports, etc.	0	1	2	3
Is hard to please	0	1	2	3
Says there is no point to things	0	1	2	3
Complains a lot	0	1	2	3

Social isolation

Is sullen and uncommunicative (especially with adults)	0	1	2	3
Will not willingly join in family or peer group activities	0	1	2	3
Stays alone in his or her room for long periods of time	0	1	2	3
Is excessively absorbed by music, computer games, cartoons, comics, etc.	0	1	2	3
Does not contact friends out of school	0	1	2	3
Thinks people are deliberately trying to upset or annoy him or her	0	1	2	3
Reluctant to attend school	0	1	2	3
Says nothing is wrong when asked	0	1	2	3

Peer group dependence

Engages in risky exploits with peers	0	1	2	3
Seems to enjoy being with peers, but is sullen and uncommunicative with adults	0	1	2	3
Disobeys adult limits on behavior	0	1	2	3
Has excessive need to be with friends	0	1	2	3
Is attention seeking and disruptive at school	0	1	2	3

Changes in energy levels

Seems to be tired most of the time	0	1	2	3
Is often lethargic and slow to respond	0	1	2	3
Is often agitated and restless	0	1	2	3

Disturbed eating or sleeping patterns

Has difficulty in getting to sleep or staying asleep	0	1	2	3
Sleeps an excessive amount or at unusual times	0	1	2	3
Eats much less than usual, not interested in food	0	1	2	3
Eats an excessive amount but may not be selective	0	1	2	3
Uses alcohol or drugs to excess	0	1	2	3

Poor concentration

Often seems indecisive	0	1	2	3
Often seems forgetful	0	1	2	3
Is often poorly organized	0	1	2	3
Often seems vague and inattentive	0	1	2	3

Low self-esteem

Does not seem to expect success	0	1	2	3
Says he or she is stupid, dumb, etc.	0	1	2	3

Finds it hard to accept criticism	0	1	2	3
Finds it hard to accept praise or affection	0	1	2	3
Says he or she would be better off dead	0	1	2	3
Says parents prefer or favor other children in family	0	1	2	3
Says teachers prefer or favor other students in class	0	1	2	3
Is inappropriately apologetic or excessively guilty about minor issues	0	1	2	3

Preoccupation with negative, violent, or morbid ideas

Draws and writes on negative, violent, or morbid topics	0	1	2	3
Talks about suicide (in general or in relation to himself or herself)	0	1	2	3
Seems overly interested in songs, news items, or films about violence and death	0	1	2	3
Has taken risks that could be suicidal	0	1	2	3

Family history

Family history of Depression or other mental illness	Yes	No	Don't know

Additional comments and observations:

DEPRESSION

Characteristics of Depression

Children and adolescents who are depressed can seem sad, withdrawn, and clearly depressed. They may resist inquiries about how they feel and say that there is nothing wrong, or they may complain of negative feelings such as boredom or loneliness rather than Depression. Students with Depression are often withdrawn and tend to isolate themselves, especially from close interpersonal contact. However, a student with Depression can also be irritable, disruptive, angry, inattentive, and very agitated.

Loss of energy and low motivation are strongly characteristic of Depression. Poor concentration is also a very strong characteristic of Depression, in both children and adults. The student with Depression may lose interest in success and say that he or she does not care about punishments or rewards. It is easy to assume that the student is simply lazy, disinterested, or noncompliant.

Some depressed students tend to gravitate toward their peer groups and put up a facade of cheerful outgoing behavior, displaying an excessive "party mood." To adults, the same student may be sullen, disrespectful, disruptive, and bad tempered.

Students with depression often have disturbances in their sleep patterns (generally finding it difficult to sleep, occasionally sleeping too much). Eating patterns may also show symptoms of depression, either in loss of appetite or indiscriminate comfort eating.

The student with Depression tends to think in a very negative way and may contemplate or carry out self-harming behavior.

Some students with Depression may become overly concerned about their physical health, making constant complaints about minor aches and pains that do not prove to have any organic origin.

Causes of Depression

It is known that irregularities in the chemicals in the brain, which are called neurotransmitters, are implicated in Depression. Depression can therefore occur without any events acting as a trigger.

Children and adolescents do of course sometimes experience very sad or traumatic events. There will be a natural period of grief or distress. Depression is diagnosed when the sad or negative feelings continue beyond the expected recovery time after such an event.

Other Conditions With Characteristics Similar to Depression

Attention-Deficit Disorder (Inattentive Type)

Students who have the inattentive form of Attention-Deficit Disorder may often seem low in motivation and energy and "in a world of their own."

Attention-Deficit/Hyperactivity Disorder

Students with Attention-Deficit/Hyperactivity Disorder can also be irritable and have a low frustration tolerance.

Oppositional Defiant Disorder

Negative, depressed mood can be an intrinsic part of Oppositional Defiant Disorder. The two conditions can also occur in parallel.

Child Abuse

Children who have been abused will also appear to be depressed. They may indeed have this clinical condition as part of their ongoing reaction to an abusive situation.

Ill Health

Children who have a medical condition (perhaps not diagnosed) can also appear to be depressed. For instance, a child who has a sleep disorder, severe anemia, or some other debilitating medical condition will seem low in motivation and flat in mood and may well present in a depressed state.

Disorders or Difficulties That May Accompany Depression

Depression and Anxiety

Some children and adolescents who are depressed also have an Anxiety Disorder.

Professionals Who May Be Involved

Teachers

The classroom teacher will of course be of primary importance in recognizing the student with depressed mood. The teacher may need to be particularly vigilant with regard to the student's irritability or tendency to withdraw and the way in which this impacts the student's socialization and overall well-being.

Psychologists, Student Counselors, or Psychiatrists

A psychologist, student counselor, or psychiatrist is likely to be involved if the student's Depression significantly impairs social, academic, or other important areas of functioning. Counseling and medication are likely treatment options.

Action Plans for Students With Depression

- Ensure that any student who seems to be low in motivation, irritable, cranky, or difficult is considered as a student with possible Depression. A student's lack of application and negative mood can mistakenly be thought to be a motivational problem.
- The student's negative or irritable mood may well impact his or her socialization, and action may be needed to support the student. For instance, peer group frictions and conflicts may erupt in the schoolyard if the student is irritable and negative. The student may be better accommodated in a small group of supportive peers taking part in an activity that is monitored by an adult.

- Low motivation and lack of interest and enthusiasm will, of course, impact schoolwork, and here the classroom teacher will need to be aware of the issues underlying the student's poor performance in daily schoolwork. It is inappropriate to punish a depressed student for poor quality or quantity of work.
- Communicate promptly with parents if you have any concerns about a student who seems to be depressed.
- Arrange for appropriate further professional advice with regard to any student who appears to be depressed.
- Ensure that the student with Depression has supportive, positive experiences during school hours. Allow leeway with regard to work completion and give encouragement and support.
- Encourage a positive mood by showing how to interpret situations positively and how to deal with negatives constructively.
- Recognize that the student with Depression probably does not have the capacity to cheer up by willpower or wishful thinking. Depression is characterized by intractable negative mood, which is often very difficult to lift voluntarily.
- Find time to make personal contact with the student so that he or she understands that you are supportive and aware that he or she is going through a tough patch.
- Be vigilant for any signs of severe Depression, including talk of self-harm.
- Be particularly aware of the content of the student's artwork and written language. Some depressed students express their darkest thoughts through drawing or writing.
- Recognize that Depression does not have a logical basis, so that the student may, to an outsider, have everything necessary to feel happy and confident, but still feel very negative and depressed.
- Ensure that the student's classroom environment is as positive and supportive as possible. It is of course particularly important for the student with Depression that the class members all give each other mutual support and avoid negatives.
- Address any issues that may be contributing to the student's negative, depressed feelings. Make sure that the student is not being harassed or victimized in any way. (Students who are depressed are particularly vulnerable to the antisocial behavior of others.)
- Use positive, uplifting, and inspiring stories, art, and music to help counteract depressed feelings.

RECOMMENDED FURTHER READING

**Promoting Positive Thinking: Building Children's Self-Esteem,
Self-Confidence and Optimism**
Author: Glynis Hannell
Date of publication: 2004
Publisher: David Fulton
ISBN: 184312257X

The Childhood Depression Sourcebook
Author: Jeffrey A. Miller
Date of publication: 1999
Publisher: McGraw-Hill/Contemporary Books
ISBN: 0737300019

**Helping Sensitive and Difficult Children: What You Can Do
About Childhood Depression and Anxiety**
Author: Steven Stritt
Date of publication: 2003
Publisher: Xlibris
ISBN: 1401057918

Childhood Depression: School-Based Intervention
Author: Kevin D. Stark
Date of publication: 1990
Publisher: Guilford Press
ISBN: 0898622360

**Help Me, I'm Sad: Recognizing, Treating, and Preventing
Childhood Depression**
Authors: Lynne S. Duman (contributor), David G. Fassier
Date of publication: 1997
Publisher: Viking Press
ASIN: 0670865478

REFERENCES FOR DEPRESSION

American Psychiatric Association. (1994). *Diagnostic and statistical manual of mental disorders* (4th ed.).Washington, DC: Author.

Cichetti, D., & Cohen, D. J. (Eds.). (1995). *Developmental psychopathology: Risk, disorder and adaptation.* New York: John Wiley & Sons.

Garber, J., & Robinson, N. S. (1997). Cognitive vulnerability in children at risk of depression. *Cognition and Emotion, 11,* 619–635.

Gotlib, I. H., & Hammen, C. L. (1992). *Psychological aspects of depression: Towards a cognitive-interpersonal integration.* New York: John Wiley & Sons.

Kovacs, M. (1985). The children's depression inventory. *Psychopharmacology, 21,* 995–1000.

Nolen-Hoeksema, S., Girgus, J. S., & Seligman, M. E. P. (1992). Predictors and consequences of childhood depressive symptoms. *Journal of Abnormal Psychology, 101,* 405–422.

Rutter, M., Izard, C. E., & Read, P. B. (Eds.). (1986). *Depression in young people: Developmental and clinical perspectives.* New York: Guilford Press.

Sparrow, S. S., Balla, D. A., & Cicchetti, D. V. (2000). *Comprehensive psychological and psychoeducational assessment of children and adolescents: A developmental approach.* Boston: Allyn & Bacon.

Toth, D. C. S. L. (Ed.). (1992). *Rochester Symposium of Developmental Psychopathology: Developmental perspectives on depression.* New York: University of Rochester Press.

World Health Organization. (2000). *ICIDH-2: International classification of functioning, disability and health.* Geneva, Switzerland: Author.

THE CONDUCT DISORDER CHECKLIST

Glynis Hannell, BA (Hons.), MSc Registered Psychologist

Student's name _____   Date _____   Student's age _____

Name of person completing checklist _____

Relationship to student _____

Each item that applies to the child or adolescent should be checked off using the following rating scale.

0 Not at all, does not apply
1 Mild, sometimes observed, applies to some extent
2 Moderate, often observed, certainly applies
3 Severe, frequently observed, strongly applies

*Please use **0** to indicate that an item has been considered and does not apply. If the **0** is not checked, it is not clear if the item has been overlooked.*

Socially inappropriate behavior

Has little empathy or concern for other people	0	1	2	3
Bullies or intimidates others	0	1	2	3
Associates with other antisocial youngsters	0	1	2	3
Is intolerant of minority groups	0	1	2	3
Is outspoken and rude	0	1	2	3
Does not respect other's rights (e.g., to learn, to enjoy peace and quiet)	0	1	2	3
Is a poor judge of other people, mistakenly thinks they are hostile or threatening	0	1	2	3
Engages in sexually promiscuous behavior	0	1	2	3
Shows little guilt or remorse for wrongdoing	0	1	2	3

Destructive

Deliberately spoils or destroys other people's possessions	0	1	2	3
Sets fires, deliberately knowing that this will cause serious damage	0	1	2	3
Vandalizes public property (graffiti, smashing glass)	0	1	2	3

Disrespectful of adult authority

Ignores parental rules or requests	0	1	2	3
Ignores school rules	0	1	2	3
Breaks the law	0	1	2	3
Runs away from home	0	1	2	3

Is truant from school	0	1	2	3
Does not comply with punishments	0	1	2	3
Is frequently suspended or expelled from school	0	1	2	3
Ignores requests by persons in authority (e.g., bus driver, traffic warden, etc.)	0	1	2	3
Ridicules adults in authority (e.g., public figures)	0	1	2	3

Physically aggressive or cruel

Often starts fights	0	1	2	3
Uses physical force or a weapon to intimidate victim	0	1	2	3
Physically aggressive if upset or annoyed	0	1	2	3
Cruel to animals	0	1	2	3
Cruel to people younger or weaker than himself or herself	0	1	2	3
Enjoys cruel, sadistic, or violent films or games	0	1	2	3
Talks aggressively or threatens violence	0	1	2	3
Drives in an aggressive and dangerous manner	0	1	2	3

Deceitful and dishonest

Lies to adults	0	1	2	3
Lies to peers	0	1	2	3
Invents or exaggerates stories about himself, herself, or others	0	1	2	3
Breaks promises	0	1	2	3
Steals from family or friends	0	1	2	3
Steals from shops, school, or other organizations	0	1	2	3
Steals cars and drives them recklessly	0	1	2	3
Breaks into premises and steals or vandalizes	0	1	2	3
Forges parent's signature	0	1	2	3
Destroys documents that incriminate him or her (e.g., letter from school to parent)	0	1	2	3
Blames others and does not accept responsibility	0	1	2	3
Incriminates others for his or her own advantage, makes false accusations	0	1	2	3
Feigns ignorance when asked for the truth	0	1	2	3
Covers up for friends who are behaving inappropriately	0	1	2	3

Drug and alcohol abuse

Uses illegal drugs	0	1	2	3
Deals in illegal drugs	0	1	2	3
Drinks alcohol or smokes cigarettes while underage	0	1	2	3
Drinks excessive alcohol	0	1	2	3

Difficult at home

Often angry and uncooperative	0	1	2	3
Secretive and often absent from home	0	1	2	3
Particularly aggressive to a specific person (e.g., mother or younger sibling)	0	1	2	3
Demanding and intimidating, must have needs met	0	1	2	3
Does not communicate positively	0	1	2	3
Does not fulfill responsibilities	0	1	2	3
Lacks warmth and empathy for family members	0	1	2	3
Acts tough but is emotionally very immature	0	1	2	3

Family history

Other family members have behavioral or mental health problems	Yes	No	Don't know

Additional comments and observations:

CONDUCT DISORDER

Characteristics of Conduct Disorder

Conduct Disorder is marked by a major disturbance in the student's behavior and relationship with others. A student with Conduct Disorder will show frequent antisocial, disruptive, and delinquent behavior, often leading to law breaking and sanctions from authority figures (suspension or expulsion from school or a period of detention through the juvenile justice system). The student may damage property and exhibit aggression, violence, deceitfulness, and other socially unacceptable behaviors.

The student with Conduct Disorder will often have impaired empathy for other people and may particularly target weak or vulnerable adults or peers with intimidation, aggression, or other antisocial acts.

The student with Conduct Disorder is more likely than others to be involved with illegal drugs, weapons, or associated activities.

Causes of Conduct Disorder

Family dysfunction is often implicated in Conduct Disorder, in which disrupted or unsatisfactory parent-child relationships may disturb normal emotional and social development. Parents may themselves have mental health or psychosocial difficulties, such as drug addiction. Lack of appropriate supervision, inconsistent discipline including arbitrary and harsh punishments, child abuse, and frequent changes of caregivers all contribute to the emergence of Conduct Disorder. Association with an antisocial and delinquent peer group may maintain and increase the student's inappropriate behavior.

Studies show that there is both a genetic and an environmental basis for Conduct Disorder, and in many situations a student with a predisposition to Conduct Disorder may also be in an environment that is conducive to the development of the disorder.

Other Conditions With Characteristics
Similar to Conduct Disorder

Oppositional Defiant Disorder

Oppositional Defiant Disorder shares some characteristics with Conduct Disorder in that both conditions involve noncompliance and oppositional behavior. Conduct Disorder is a more severe behavioral disturbance and involves many more negative characteristics than does Oppositional Defiant Disorder alone.

Disorders or Difficulties That
May Accompany Conduct Disorder

Conduct Disorder and Attention-Deficit/Hyperactivity Disorder

These two conditions are often seen in tandem, and most students with Conduct Disorder also have Attention-Deficit/Hyperactivity Disorder. It is important to note that the reverse is not true—the majority of students with Attention-Deficit Disorder do not have Conduct Disorder.

Conduct Disorder and Learning Difficulties

Students with Conduct Disorder are likely to have lower than average intelligence, poorer academic skills, and more specific difficulties with learning than their peers.

Professionals Who May Be Involved

Teachers

The student may be part of a general class, in which case the general-class teacher will have a primary role in working with the student in class, usually with the support of a specialist educator with expertise in behavior management.

*Counselors, Behavior Management
Specialists, and Special Educational Facilities*

The student will almost certainly need specialist support from student counselors or behavior management specialists. The student may be placed in a special educational facility for either short-term or long-term behavioral management and support. In this case, specialist educators will certainly be involved.

Psychiatrists and Psychologists

A psychiatrist or psychologist will also likely be involved in supporting the student and professional colleagues working with the student.

Social Workers

A social worker may be involved in working with the student and his or her family to address parenting and other issues.

Probation Officers and Youth Workers Attached to the Justice System

A probation officer or other professional from a law enforcement agency may also be involved with regard to modifying the student's antisocial and illegal behaviors.

Action Plans for Supporting
a Student With Conduct Disorder

- Recognize that the student with Conduct Disorder is often the product of a dysfunctional family or community group in which abuse, neglect, and inappropriate parenting may have played a significant role in the student's development.
- Arrange for appropriate professional advice for behavior management and family support.
- Ensure that the teachers assigned to teach the student are capable of maintaining the student's compliance and cooperation in the classroom.

Avoid placing the student with teachers who do not have effective control of their classes, as the student with Conduct Disorder is likely to become a major disruption.

- Anticipate that students with Conduct Disorder are likely to have genuine learning difficulties along with their behavioral problems, and plan an appropriate program to suit the students' learning needs.
- Give firm, consistent, and fair behavioral boundaries and implement them quickly and confidently.
- Recognize and value the student's positive qualities to help build his or her self-respect.
- Give opportunities for the student to show empathy and compassion in a supported and supervised environment. For example, students with Conduct Disorder may prove to be caring and responsible when caring for animals or younger children.
- Make a particular effort to build up a positive relationship with the student so that you can keep the channels of communication open.
- Ensure that consequences for unacceptable behavior have a very direct and tangible link with what the student has done. If the student has defaced school property, then the appropriate punishment is to restore the item to original condition or do enough hours of community service to earn enough to replace the damaged item. If the student has intimidated or harassed another child or adolescent, then he or she should face that person to apologize and offer some form of recompense.

RECOMMENDED FURTHER READING

All the Best Answers for the Worst Kid Problems: Anti Social Youth and Conduct Disorders
Author: Ruth Herman Wells
Date of publication: 2003
Publisher: Youth Change
ISBN: 1891881280

The Defiant Child: A Parent's Guide to Oppositional Defiant Disorder
Author: Douglas A. Riley
Date of publication: 1997
Publisher: Taylor
ISBN: 0878339639

From Defiance to Cooperation: Real Solutions for Transforming the Angry, Defiant, Discouraged Child
Author: John F. Taylor
Date of publication: 2001
Publisher: Prima Lifestyles
ISBN: 0761529551

Treating the Disruptive Adolescent: Finding the Real Self Behind Oppositional Defiant Disorders
Author: Eduardo M. Bustamante
Date of publication: 2000
Publisher: Jason Aronson
ISBN: 0765702355

Educating Oppositional and Defiant Children
Authors: Philip S. Hall, Nancy D. Hall
Date of publication: 2003
Publisher: Association for Supervision & Curriculum Development
ISBN: 0871207613

Winning Cooperation from Your Child: A Comprehensive Method to Stop Defiant and Aggressive Behavior in Children (Developments in Clinical Psychiatry)
Author: Kenneth Wenning
Date of publication: 1999
Publisher: Jason Aronson
ISBN: 0765702312

Handbook of Disruptive Behavior Disorders
Authors: Herbert C. Quay, Anne E. Hogan
Date of publication: 1999
Publisher: Kluwer Academic
ISBN: 0306459744, all editions

REFERENCES FOR CONDUCT DISORDER

Achenbach, T. M. (1991). *Manual for the child behavior checklist.* Burlington: Department of Psychiatry, University of Vermont.

American Psychiatric Association. (1994). *Diagnostic and statistical manual of mental disorders* (4th ed.). Washington, DC: Author.

Cichetti, D., & Cohen, D. J. (Eds.). (1995). *Developmental psychopathology: Risk, disorder and adaptation.* New York: John Wiley & Sons.

Harris, J., Tyre, C., & Wilkinson, C. (1993). Using the Child Behavior Checklist in ordinary primary schools. *British Journal of Educational Psychology, 63,* 245–260.

Hoge, R. D., & Andrews, D. A. (1992). Assessing conduct problems in the classroom. *Clinical Psychology Review, 12,* 1–20.

Rutter, M., Taylor, E., & Hersov, L. (Eds.). (1994). *Child and adolescent psychiatry: Modern approaches.* Cambridge, MA: Blackwell Science.

Walker, H. M. (1995). *The acting out child: Coping with classroom disruption* (2nd ed.). Boston: Allyn & Bacon.

World Health Organization. (2000). *ICIDH-2: International classification of functioning, disability and health.* Geneva, Switzerland: Author.

THE OPPOSITIONAL DEFIANT DISORDER CHECKLIST

Glynis Hannell, BA (Hons.), MSc Registered Psychologist

Student's name _____ Date _____ Student's age _____

Name of person completing checklist _____

Relationship to student _____

Each item that applies to the child or adolescent should be checked off using the following rating scale.

0 Not at all, does not apply
1 Mild, sometimes observed, applies to some extent
2 Moderate, often observed, certainly applies
3 Severe, frequently observed, strongly applies

*Please use **0** to indicate that an item has been considered and does not apply. If the **0** is not checked, it is not clear if the item has been overlooked.*

Difficult to discipline

Refuses to comply with reasonable requests	0	1	2	3
Deliberately disobeys rules	0	1	2	3
Finds loopholes in rules	0	1	2	3
Does not seem to care if privileges or favorite things are removed	0	1	2	3
Does not like to reveal that punishments are hurting	0	1	2	3
Does not like to show that they are pleased with rewards	0	1	2	3
Becomes defiant and disobedient when criticized or punished	0	1	2	3
Becomes aggressive and violent when criticized or punished	0	1	2	3
Makes threats to try to stop adults disciplining him or her	0	1	2	3
Blames others for his or her own wrongdoing	0	1	2	3
Highly indignant about own innocence if blamed	0	1	2	3
Very persistent if ignored, will escalate behavior until adults respond	0	1	2	3
Justifies behavior by saying rules, requests, etc., were unreasonable	0	1	2	3

Difficult to please

Is unwilling to show pleasure in gifts or outings	0	1	2	3
Spoils family trips by constant complaining	0	1	2	3
Is reluctant to say what he or she wants	0	1	2	3
Does not want what is offered, wants something different	0	1	2	3

Rejects what adults thought would be a treat	0	1	2	3
Changes preferences (asks for one thing and then rejects it when it is given)	0	1	2	3

Argues with adults

Often says the opposite of what adults say	0	1	2	3
Argues endlessly, even when obviously wrong	0	1	2	3
Tries to make adult look at fault	0	1	2	3
Says or does something and then denies it	0	1	2	3

Lack of respect for adults

Uses body language and facial expression to defy adults	0	1	2	3
Scoffs at what adults say	0	1	2	3
Talks about adults in a disrespectful way	0	1	2	3
Will not accept adult authority	0	1	2	3
Plays adults off against one another	0	1	2	3
Is very demanding of adults; expects them to accept orders	0	1	2	3
Tries to manipulate others to undermine adults	0	1	2	3

Often deliberately annoys people

Deliberately annoys siblings or peers	0	1	2	3
Openly defies rules when adults are watching	0	1	2	3
Often tests limits	0	1	2	3

Easily annoyed

Is very touchy and easily annoyed	0	1	2	3
Views simple accidents as deliberate provocations	0	1	2	3
Gets very angry if siblings or peers retaliate to his or her provocation	0	1	2	3
Is easily irritated if things do not work properly	0	1	2	3
Is very sensitive (e.g., "hates" an everyday noise such as a sibling sniffing)	0	1	2	3

Angry or resentful

Loses temper very quickly over minor matters	0	1	2	3
Takes general criticism very personally	0	1	2	3
Sees personal accusations where none were intended	0	1	2	3
Holds grudges for a long time	0	1	2	3
Sulks for a long time after an upset	0	1	2	3

time and effort into developing new, more appropriate and acceptable behaviors.

- Evaluate the trigger points for the student's oppositional defiant behavior, so that all parties understand what triggers the inappropriate behavior and what types of management styles and environmental factors minimize the problems.

- Managing Oppositional Defiant Disorder is very much an exercise in networking and collaboration. It is important that all important adults in the child's or adolescent's life coordinate their efforts so that consistency is ensured.

- Students with Oppositional Defiant Disorder are often children or adolescents to whom control and preserving personal dignity are very important issues. Explore ways in which the student might be given responsibility and control and preserve their personal dignity in appropriate ways.

- Wherever possible, behavioral management needs to be dealt with in private so that the student is not backed into a position in front of peers, where the only way to preserve their image is to continue to defy and oppose the adult. Students who have cultivated an image as defiant and oppositional are very unlikely to agree to a "deal" in front of their peers.

- Adults need to prioritize, so that oppositional defiant students have ample opportunity to feel that they are making their own decisions about issues such as what clothing they wear or what food they eat.

- Issues that are matters of life or death, or that have serious safety or interpersonal risks attached to them, need to be dealt with by the use of clear boundaries and explicit consequences. Use words such as *top priority, red alert,* and *Code 1* to signal to the students that the issue is of critical importance. Make sure that the students know that these issues are not negotiable and that adults will do whatever is necessary to ensure that the student complies with these rules.

- Be prepared to put in time and effort to develop a good rapport with the student who is oppositional and defiant. Often these students are seeking to build their image and self-respect by their inappropriate behavior. Let them know that you are prepared to have a good opinion of them and have confidence in them.

- Invest time in building compliance and cooperation. Be there to follow through quickly. Refuse to engage in endless arguments, but use your energy to devise alternatives that offer the student acceptable (often face-saving) options.

- Teach the student that quick compliance over small matters leads to a win-win situation. Give reward cards or tokens for a quick response, maybe with a bonus for a good attitude. Give rewards that show they are earning your trust and as a result are being given responsibilities. Students who accumulate tokens or cards are given privileges that are normally restricted to older students, such as going to the office without a partner, being allowed to walk with friends to the lunch room rather than in a line, or being allowed to go into an out-of-bounds area or borrow school sports equipment at lunch and recess.

- It is very important that appropriate behavior is teamed with a positive consequence to counterbalance the fact that inappropriate choices are followed through with negative consequences. However, this needs to be carefully handled, as students with oppositional defiant behavior tend to resist showing pleasure in treats or distress at punishments, so conventional rewards do not always work. Control is important to the student with oppositional defiant behavior, so rewards that give choices and control are often effective. Say, for example, "It's your choice. Finish this task then you can choose whether or not you will do the math assignment. If you choose not to do the task, then I choose not to drive you to the sports center tonight. It's up to you."

- Adults must be in a position to carry through both positive and negative consequences, and these must happen quickly after the student has made a choice. Never promise positive consequences or threaten negative ones that you cannot deliver immediately after the student has made a choice. Always follow through.

- In most areas of the student's life, there are issues that need some adult constraint but that also have scope for some student choice. In this situation, the oppositional defiant student is given a range of choices within the parameters set by adults, for example, a piece of work may need to be done by a certain date, but the actual timing of when the work is done is negotiable with the student.

- The important thing in all of the above is that the student is given a clear description of desirable and appropriate behavior and a positive consequence for demonstrating that behavior. The student remains in control of the choices, but the adults remain in control of the consequences.

RECOMMENDED FURTHER READING

The Defiant Child: A Parent's Guide to Oppositional Defiant Disorder
Author: Douglas A. Riley
Date of publication: 1997
Publisher: Taylor
ISBN: 0878339639

From Defiance to Cooperation: Real Solutions for Transforming the Angry, Defiant, Discouraged Child
Author: John F. Taylor
Date of publication: 2001
Publisher: Prima Lifestyles
ISBN: 0761529551

Treating the Disruptive Adolescent: Finding the Real Self Behind Oppositional Defiant Disorders
Author: Eduardo M. Bustamante
Date of publication: 2000
Publisher: Jason Aronson
ISBN: 0765702355

Educating Oppositional and Defiant Children
Authors: Philip S. Hall, Nancy D. Hall
Date of publication: 2003
Publisher: Association for Supervision & Curriculum Development
ISBN: 0871207613

**Winning Cooperation From Your Child: A Comprehensive
Method to Stop Defiant and Aggressive Behavior in Children
(Developments in Clinical Psychiatry)**
Author: Kenneth Wenning
Date of publication: 1999
Publisher: Jason Aronson
ISBN: 0765702312

Handbook of Disruptive Behavior Disorders
Authors: Herbert C. Quay, Anne E. Hogan
Date of publication: 1999
Publisher: Kluwer Academic
ISBN: 0306459744, all editions

REFERENCES FOR OPPOSITIONAL DEFIANT DISORDER

Achenbach, T. M. (1991). *Manual for the child behavior checklist.* Burlington: Department of Psychiatry, University of Vermont.

American Psychiatric Association. (1994). *Diagnostic and statistical manual of mental disorders* (4th ed.).Washington, DC: Author.

Cichetti, D., & Cohen, D. J. (Eds.). (1995). *Developmental psychopathology: Risk, disorder and adaptation.* New York: John Wiley & Sons.

Harris, J., Tyre, C., & Wilkinson, C. (1993). Using the Child Behavior Checklist in ordinary primary schools. *British Journal of Educational Psychology, 63,* 245–260.

Hoge, R. D., & Andrews, D. A. (1992). Assessing conduct problems in the classroom. *Clinical Psychology Review, 12,* 1–20.

Rutter, M., Taylor, E., & Hersov, L. (Eds.). (1994). *Child and adolescent psychiatry: Modern approaches.* Cambridge, MA: Blackwell Science.

Sparrow, S. S., Balla, D. A., & Cicchetti, D. V. (2000). *Comprehensive psychological and psychoeducational assessment of children and adolescents: A developmental approach.* Boston: Allyn & Bacon.

Stroff, D. M., Breiling, J., & Maser, J. D. (Eds.). (1997). *Handbook of antisocial behavior.* New York: John Wiley & Sons.

Walker, H. M. (1995). *The acting out child. Coping with classroom disruption* (2nd ed.). Boston: Allyn & Bacon.

World Health Organization. (2000). *ICIDH-2: International classification of functioning, disability and health.* Geneva, Switzerland: Author.

Spiteful or vindictive

Will deliberately spoil others' fun	0	1	2	3
Will retaliate in a spiteful or vindictive way	0	1	2	3
Ridicules success or popularity in others	0	1	2	3
Spoils surprises or secrets	0	1	2	3

Associated problems

Has Attention-Deficit/Hyperactivity Disorder	0	1	2	3
Has learning difficulties	0	1	2	3
Has communication difficulties	0	1	2	3

Family history

Other family members have a history of Oppositional Defiant Disorder	Yes	No	Don't know
Other family members have had behavioral or mental health problems	Yes	No	Don't know

Additional comments and observations:

OPPOSITIONAL DEFIANT DISORDER

Characteristics of Oppositional Defiant Disorder

The child or adolescent who has Oppositional Defiant Disorder has marked difficulties in dealing with interpersonal interactions, particularly with adults. They may seem to deliberately provoke conflict by contradicting what is said, resisting reasonable requests, and ignoring established rules and conventions of behavior. The student with Oppositional Defiant Disorder may seem to go out of his or her way to challenge adults over both minor and major issues.

The oppositional component of the disorder means that the student opposes what would normally be seen as acceptable by other students who do not have the disorder. For instance, an oppositional student might make it clear that he or she dislikes something that all other students are clearly enjoying, to the point of disrupting the event.

The defiant component of the disorder indicates that the student is prepared to defy reasonable requests, rules, and instructions. For instance, the student might overtly break a known rule while knowing that adults are watching.

Another mark of Oppositional Defiant Disorder is intensive, rapid shifts of mood leading to the student suddenly becoming very angry over minor provocations.

Some degree of oppositional defiant behavior is normal at certain stages of development. In early childhood, there is a stage (usually between 2 and 3 years of age) in which children typically become noncompliant as they are beginning to learn to handle the complexities of interpersonal relationships and to manage the inevitable restrictions that are placed on them.

In adolescents, some degree of oppositional behavior may be seen as normal, and it is part of the process of the student creating his or her own unique individuality, separate from their parents.

Disorders That Have Characteristics Similar to Oppositional Defiant Disorder

Asperger Syndrome

Students with Asperger Syndrome may appear to be oppositional and defiant in situations in which their rigid and inflexible mind-set and their poor social skills are not correctly diagnosed as part of the Autism Spectrum Disorder.

Depression

Students with Depression are often negative, do not seem to care about rewards or punishments, and may be withdrawn and noncompliant. They may also be irritable and agitated and behave inappropriately.

Conduct Disorder

Conduct Disorder is a more extreme behavior disorder than Oppositional Defiant Disorder and brings with it aggression toward people and animals, destruction of property, vandalism, theft, or dishonesty. Generally speaking, all of the features of Oppositional Defiant Disorder are included within Conduct Disorder, but Conduct Disorder is a more severe and widespread behavioral problem.

Intellectually Gifted Students

Intellectually gifted students placed in a situation in which their intellectual capacities are not recognized and channeled can sometimes appear to be oppositional and defiant in the way that they will challenge adults' opinions and decisions.

Mental Retardation (Cognitive Disability)

Children and adolescents with intellectual disability may become oppositional or defiant, particularly if their intellectual disability is not fully understood. Their difficulties with complying with reasonable requests and their limitations with interpersonal skills may be seen as willful, rather than as an intrinsic part of their intellectual disability.

Language Impairment

Some students with Language Impairment may also seem oppositional or defiant because they have problems in receptive language. This means that they do not fully understand what is said to them, and they may have difficulties formulating their answers. If this is viewed as a behavior problem, the child may become increasingly frustrated and behave inappropriately.

Disorders or Difficulties That May Accompany Oppositional Defiant Disorder

Oppositional Defiant Disorder and Attention-Deficit Disorder

This is a common combination. It may be that each disorder is an entity in itself, or it may be that the Attention-Deficit Disorder triggers Oppositional Defiant Disorder in particular environmental circumstances. For instance, a student with Attention-Deficit Disorder may have had many years of inconsistent discipline for impulsive behavior and may gradually acquire an oppositional or defiant style of interacting with adults.

Attention-Deficit Disorder brings with it a tendency to instability of mood, impulsiveness, and high reactivity. These features are also common characteristics of Oppositional Defiant Disorder.

Causes of Oppositional Defiant Disorder

The causes of Oppositional Defiant Disorder are complex, and each individual has his or her own set of causative factors. Certainly innate personality traits will play their part. Some children are simply born with a greater tendency to be determined and individualistic than others. It some situations, these underlying personality traits will be expressed as oppositional and defiant behaviors; in other situations, these characteristics may become positive attributes in the adult world.

Oppositional Defiant Disorder is associated with adult discipline that is inconsistent, fluctuating from excessively punitive and harsh to ineffective, overindulgent, or neglectful.

Students with Oppositional Defiant Disorder often use their noncompliant behavior to disguise or compensate for feelings of personal inadequacy or their lack of alternative, socially acceptable ways of earning prestige and self-respect.

Oppositional Defiant Disorder can be associated with family dysfunction, although it is very important to note that not all children experiencing the same family situation will develop oppositional defiant behaviors. There seems to be a complex interplay of personality and situation.

A strong role model in an older sibling, parent, or other important person in the child's life can also increase the likelihood of similar behaviors being expressed in the student. An innate tendency to be oppositional and defiant may be exacerbated by a family or community culture in which such tendencies are modeled, supported, or encouraged.

Professionals Who May Be Involved

Teachers

Teachers and special educators will of course provide primary care at school.

Counselors, Behavior Management Specialists, and Social Workers

School counselors and behavior management specialists may be involved to support classroom teachers and parents with regard to general management issues.

Psychologists and Psychiatrists

A child and adolescent psychiatrist or psychologist is likely to have a significant role when looking at the causal factors and appropriate treatment and management for the student's Oppositional Defiant Disorder.

Action Plans for Students With Oppositional Defiant Disorder

- Arrange an appropriate assessment with a psychologist or child and adolescent psychiatrist with expertise in diagnosing behavioral disorders. It is important to eliminate the possibility that the student has another underlying disorder (Mental Retardation, Asperger Syndrome, Attention-Deficit Disorder, etc.) before treating the student with a behavioral approach.
- Recognize that the student with oppositional defiant behavior may have little or no experience using appropriate behaviors, so his or her repertoire of alternatives may be extremely limited. As well as working toward eliminating undesirable behaviors, it is critically important to put

time and effort into developing new, more appropriate and acceptable behaviors.

- Evaluate the trigger points for the student's oppositional defiant behavior, so that all parties understand what triggers the inappropriate behavior and what types of management styles and environmental factors minimize the problems.

- Managing Oppositional Defiant Disorder is very much an exercise in networking and collaboration. It is important that all important adults in the child's or adolescent's life coordinate their efforts so that consistency is ensured.

- Students with Oppositional Defiant Disorder are often children or adolescents to whom control and preserving personal dignity are very important issues. Explore ways in which the student might be given responsibility and control and preserve their personal dignity in appropriate ways.

- Wherever possible, behavioral management needs to be dealt with in private so that the student is not backed into a position in front of peers, where the only way to preserve their image is to continue to defy and oppose the adult. Students who have cultivated an image as defiant and oppositional are very unlikely to agree to a "deal" in front of their peers.

- Adults need to prioritize, so that oppositional defiant students have ample opportunity to feel that they are making their own decisions about issues such as what clothing they wear or what food they eat.

- Issues that are matters of life or death, or that have serious safety or interpersonal risks attached to them, need to be dealt with by the use of clear boundaries and explicit consequences. Use words such as *top priority, red alert,* and *Code 1* to signal to the students that the issue is of critical importance. Make sure that the students know that these issues are not negotiable and that adults will do whatever is necessary to ensure that the student complies with these rules.

- Be prepared to put in time and effort to develop a good rapport with the student who is oppositional and defiant. Often these students are seeking to build their image and self-respect by their inappropriate behavior. Let them know that you are prepared to have a good opinion of them and have confidence in them.

- Invest time in building compliance and cooperation. Be there to follow through quickly. Refuse to engage in endless arguments, but use your energy to devise alternatives that offer the student acceptable (often face-saving) options.

- Teach the student that quick compliance over small matters leads to a win-win situation. Give reward cards or tokens for a quick response, maybe with a bonus for a good attitude. Give rewards that show they are earning your trust and as a result are being given responsibilities. Students who accumulate tokens or cards are given privileges that are normally restricted to older students, such as going to the office without a partner, being allowed to walk with friends to the lunch room rather than in a line, or being allowed to go into an out-of-bounds area or borrow school sports equipment at lunch and recess.

- It is very important that appropriate behavior is teamed with a positive consequence to counterbalance the fact that inappropriate choices are followed through with negative consequences. However, this needs to be carefully handled, as students with oppositional defiant behavior tend to resist showing pleasure in treats or distress at punishments, so conventional rewards do not always work. Control is important to the student with oppositional defiant behavior, so rewards that give choices and control are often effective. Say, for example, "It's your choice. Finish this task then you can choose whether or not you will do the math assignment. If you choose not to do the task, then I choose not to drive you to the sports center tonight. It's up to you."

- Adults must be in a position to carry through both positive and negative consequences, and these must happen quickly after the student has made a choice. Never promise positive consequences or threaten negative ones that you cannot deliver immediately after the student has made a choice. Always follow through.

- In most areas of the student's life, there are issues that need some adult constraint but that also have scope for some student choice. In this situation, the oppositional defiant student is given a range of choices within the parameters set by adults, for example, a piece of work may need to be done by a certain date, but the actual timing of when the work is done is negotiable with the student.

- The important thing in all of the above is that the student is given a clear description of desirable and appropriate behavior and a positive consequence for demonstrating that behavior. The student remains in control of the choices, but the adults remain in control of the consequences.

RECOMMENDED FURTHER READING

The Defiant Child: A Parent's Guide to Oppositional Defiant Disorder
Author: Douglas A. Riley
Date of publication: 1997
Publisher: Taylor
ISBN: 0878339639

From Defiance to Cooperation: Real Solutions for Transforming the Angry, Defiant, Discouraged Child
Author: John F. Taylor
Date of publication: 2001
Publisher: Prima Lifestyles
ISBN: 0761529551

Treating the Disruptive Adolescent: Finding the Real Self Behind Oppositional Defiant Disorders
Author: Eduardo M. Bustamante
Date of publication: 2000
Publisher: Jason Aronson
ISBN: 0765702355

Educating Oppositional and Defiant Children
Authors: Philip S. Hall, Nancy D. Hall
Date of publication: 2003
Publisher: Association for Supervision & Curriculum Development
ISBN: 0871207613

Winning Cooperation From Your Child: A Comprehensive
Method to Stop Defiant and Aggressive Behavior in Children
(Developments in Clinical Psychiatry)
Author: Kenneth Wenning
Date of publication: 1999
Publisher: Jason Aronson
ISBN: 0765702312

Handbook of Disruptive Behavior Disorders
Authors: Herbert C. Quay, Anne E. Hogan
Date of publication: 1999
Publisher: Kluwer Academic
ISBN: 0306459744, all editions

REFERENCES FOR
OPPOSITIONAL DEFIANT DISORDER

Achenbach, T. M. (1991). *Manual for the child behavior checklist.* Burlington: Department of Psychiatry, University of Vermont.

American Psychiatric Association. (1994). *Diagnostic and statistical manual of mental disorders* (4th ed.).Washington, DC: Author.

Cichetti, D., & Cohen, D. J. (Eds.). (1995). *Developmental psychopathology: Risk, disorder and adaptation.* New York: John Wiley & Sons.

Harris, J., Tyre, C., & Wilkinson, C. (1993). Using the Child Behavior Checklist in ordinary primary schools. *British Journal of Educational Psychology, 63,* 245–260.

Hoge, R. D., & Andrews, D. A. (1992). Assessing conduct problems in the classroom. *Clinical Psychology Review, 12,* 1–20.

Rutter, M., Taylor, E. & Hersov, L. (Eds.). (1994). *Child and adolescent psychiatry: Modern approaches.* Cambridge, MA: Blackwell Science.

Sparrow, S. S., Balla, D. A., & Cicchetti, D. V. (2000). *Comprehensive psychological and psychoeducational assessment of children and adolescents: A developmental approach.* Boston: Allyn & Bacon.

Stroff, D. M., Breiling, J., & Maser, J. D. (Eds.). (1997). *Handbook of antisocial behavior.* New York: John Wiley & Sons.

Walker, H. M. (1995). *The acting out child. Coping with classroom disruption* (2nd ed.). Boston: Allyn & Bacon.

World Health Organization. (2000). *ICIDH-2: International classification of functioning, disability and health.* Geneva, Switzerland: Author.

MENTAL RETARDATION

There is one checklist in this section:

- Mental Retardation

DEFINITION OF MENTAL RETARDATION: INDIVIDUALS WITH DISABILITIES EDUCATION ACT (IDEA)

Mental retardation means significantly subaverage general intellectual functioning, existing concurrently with deficits in adaptive behavior and manifested during the developmental period, that adversely affects a child's educational performance.

HOW TO USE THE CHECKLIST

Complete the Checklist

Fill in the administrative details at the top of the form.

Consider each item in turn. Record your subjective evaluation of the extent to which that item applies to the student.

Add any additional comments or qualifications in the space provided at the end of the questionnaire.

Interpret the Checklist

The checklist is a screening instrument, and the ratings that you have selected reflect your observations of the child or adolescent. The more items that apply to a child or adolescent, and the more frequently these items have been observed, the more likely it is that the child or adolescent has Mental Retardation (also known as Cognitive Disability). However, it is important to remember that several other conditions have similar characteristics and that specialist assessment is necessary for formal diagnosis.

For your information, descriptions of the disorders, similar conditions, and conditions that may accompany the disorder are provided.

Decide Whether to Refer for Further Assessment

The checklists will help you to decide whether to refer the student for further assessment. Guidelines are given on pages 5 and 7 for using the rating scales.

Look at the Subcategories of the Checklist

The subcategories will help you isolate any specific areas of difficulty and plan appropriate intervention strategies targeted to the student's individual needs. The action plans that follow will help give you some practical ideas for intervention strategies.

THE MENTAL RETARDATION CHECKLIST

Glynis Hannell, BA (Hons.), MSc Registered Psychologist

Student's name _____ Date _____ Student's age _____

Name of person completing checklist _____

Relationship to student _____

Each item that applies to the child or adolescent should be checked off using the following rating scale.

0 Not at all, does not apply
1 Mild, sometimes observed, applies to some extent
2 Moderate, often observed, certainly applies
3 Severe, frequently observed, strongly applies

*Please use **0** to indicate that an item has been considered and does not apply. If the **0** is not checked, it is not clear if the item has been overlooked.*

Early developmental delay

Was slow to learn to talk	0	1	2	3
Was delayed in achieving physical milestones (walking, sitting)	0	1	2	3
Was later than usual in achieving toilet training	0	1	2	3

Needs more help than usual for a child or adolescent of same age

Needs more help than usual with personal hygiene	0	1	2	3
Needs more adult guidance with regard to organization	0	1	2	3
Needs more adult supervision with basic chores such as bed making	0	1	2	3
Needs more adult supervision with regard to safety	0	1	2	3
Needs more adult supervision with managing money	0	1	2	3
Needs adult guidance with regard to sexually explicit behavior	0	1	2	3

Social difficulties

Finds it difficult to make friends of own age group	0	1	2	3
Often gets teased or bullied	0	1	2	3
Is socially naïve	0	1	2	3
Is often too trusting of others, very gullible, and easily duped	0	1	2	3
Is easily led or set up by others	0	1	2	3
Is uninhibited; does not realize when it is important to hold back	0	1	2	3

Makes inappropriate friends	0	1	2	3
Thinks someone is a friend when he or she is only an acquaintance	0	1	2	3
Believes in Santa, tooth fairy, etc., much later than peers	0	1	2	3

Immature play and recreation

Often plays with younger age group	0	1	2	3
Often likes toys, books, TV programs, or activities suitable for younger age group	0	1	2	3
Gets frustrated and confused by age-appropriate toys or games	0	1	2	3
Is physically rough or silly in organized games	0	1	2	3

Assessments indicate well below average abilities

IQ score less than 70	0	1	2	3
Scores two or more standard deviations below the mean on tests of intelligence	0	1	2	3

Additional difficulties or disorders

Speech and language less well developed than peers	0	1	2	3
Physically clumsy	0	1	2	3
Has additional difficulties or impairments, such as hearing or visual difficulties	0	1	2	3

Classroom difficulties

Restless and inattentive in group activities	0	1	2	3
Avoids schoolwork	0	1	2	3
Depends very much on others	0	1	2	3
Needs a lot of teacher attention	0	1	2	3
Gets distressed and uncooperative when tasks assigned	0	1	2	3
Does not ask for help (may not realize that he or she is on the wrong track)	0	1	2	3

Learning difficulties

Makes very slow academic progress in comparison to peers	0	1	2	3
Is significantly below standard in all curriculum areas	0	1	2	3
Needs learning broken into small stages	0	1	2	3
Needs a lot of repetition to master new learning	0	1	2	3
Needs concrete, hands-on learning experiences	0	1	2	3
Needs explicit teaching	0	1	2	3
Reading comprehension is poor even when accuracy is reasonable	0	1	2	3

Finds abstract concepts difficult	0	1	2	3
Drawing and bookwork is immature	0	1	2	3
A high level of effort does not produce expected outcomes	0	1	2	3
Seems to be falling further and further behind as time goes by	0	1	2	3

Family history

Siblings or other family members have Mental Retardation	Yes	No	Don't know

Additional comments and observations:

MENTAL RETARDATION

Mental Ratardation is also known as:

- Learning Difficulties
- Intellectual Disability
- Cognitive Impairment
- Mental Impairment

Characteristics of Mental Retardation

In the general classroom, the student with Mental Retardation will almost certainly experience significant difficulties with most learning tasks that have been set for the class. It is also likely that the student will have problems with socialization, personal organization, and general life skills problem solving.

Mental Retardation is diagnosed by the use of a standard psychometric test such as the Wechsler Intelligence Scales, the Stanford Binet, or the Kauffman Assessment Battery for Children. If the student's IQ (or similar measure) is at least two standard deviations below the mean (IQ of 70 or less), then Mental Retardation will be diagnosed if there are also commensurate impairments in adaptive skills.

There are degrees of Mental Retardation:

- Mild to Moderate Mental Retardation: IQ 70 to 50
- Severe to Profound Mental Retardation: IQ less than 50

The particular characteristics of the disability will vary, depending on its severity and the child's or adolescent's own personal characteristics. Generally speaking, the more severe the impairment, the earlier and more easily it is identified. Students with mild Mental Retardation may go through one or more years of formal schooling before they are identified.

In the early years between 3 and 9 years of age, children may be placed in the early childhood special education category or be described as having a Developmental Delay, rather than in the Mental Retardation category (see Introduction, "A Word About IDEA").This classification is made in recognition of the fact that young children's development can be very uneven in the early years.

A student with mild to moderate Mental Retardation may well mature into an adult who can achieve a reasonable degree of social and vocational independence, although he or she will perhaps need some additional support in the more complex areas of life such as management of personal finances.

On the other hand, individuals with Severe to Profound Mental Retardation are likely to be seriously impaired and to require intensive, ongoing support and assistance during their entire life span.

Causes of Mental Retardation

In approximately 30% to 40% of children and adolescents with Mental Retardation, no clear cause can be established.

Inborn errors of metabolism can be inherited. Most notable inherited causes of Mental Retardation are Fragile X Syndrome and Translocation Down's Syndrome.

Chromosomal changes in early embryonic development such as Down's Syndrome or prenatal damage due to toxins (such as excessive maternal alcohol consumption) are also significant causes of Mental Retardation.

Pregnancy and prenatal problems account for approximately 10% of children with Mental Retardation. These problems include fetal malnutrition, prematurity, hypoxia, infections, and other traumas.

Sometimes Mental Retardation is acquired after birth, particularly in situations in which there are serious infections, such as meningitis or head injuries (special education disability category traumatic brain injury) or lead poisoning.

Mental Retardation may often accompany other serious conditions, such as Autism.

It is important to note that students with Mental Retardation are at greater risk of having other mild developmental or medical difficulties, such as problems with hearing, eyesight, and general health. For some, there may be a psychosocial component that makes an additional contribution. For example, an impoverished home environment that lacks intellectual stimulation may contribute to the level of disability.

Other Conditions With Similar Characteristics to Mental Retardation

Language Impairment

Young children, particularly those with a moderate or severe Language Impairment, can present as having a Cognitive Disability or Mental Retardation. However, there is a clear distinction between those children who have global developmental delay due to Mental Retardation and those students who have language delay or Language Impairment, whereas other areas of their development are in the normal range for their age group.

Autism

Most autistic students will also have Mental Retardation. The diagnosis will depend on the nature and severity of the autistic features. If the autistic characteristics are substantial and pervasive, then the primary diagnosis will be Autism, rather than Mental Retardation. It is important to recognize that most students with Autism will also have Mental Retardation, although establishing the student's level of cognitive functioning can be very difficult in situations in which Autism is severe.

Disorders and Difficulties That May Accompany Mental Retardation

Mental Retardation and Autism

Some students with Mental Retardation will also have autistic characteristics. The two conditions can occur together, and the primary diagnosis will depend on the relative severity of the two conditions.

Mental Retardation and Attention-Deficit Disorder

Many students with Mental Retardation do also have problems with self-regulating their concentration and impulsive behavior and have Attention-Deficit Disorder along with their Mental Retardation. Making a distinction between the two conditions can be a difficult and complex diagnostic issue.

Mental Retardation can mimic the symptoms of Attention-Deficit Disorder if the student is placed in a situation in which the level of difficulty of tasks is too high or the pace of delivery of instruction is too fast. In this case, the student's inattentiveness may just be a natural response to a situation that is inappropriate to his or her needs.

Mental Retardation and Behavioral Disturbance

Students with Mental Retardation can also have a behavioral disturbance in parallel with intellectual impairments. However, Mental Retardation can exacerbate or even mimic the symptoms of Behavioral Disturbance. The student may not understand instructions or be able to do what is required. As a consequence, he or she may seem to have a Behavioral Disorder. This would be particularly likely to occur if a student with Mental Retardation has not been identified and is in a general classroom without special support or recognition of his or her disabilities.

Students with Mental Retardation often have poor social judgment and poor impulse inhibition. This may well contribute to the fact that they show symptoms of a behavioral disturbance.

Mental Retardation and Emotional Disturbance

Students with Mental Retardation may often experience marked problems in becoming integrated into their classrooms and the social networks of their peer groups. They may also experience great frustration in coping with the everyday demands of normal life. In turn, this can produce depression, anxiety, and low self-esteem.

Depression, anxiety, and other emotional disorders can also exist in parallel with Mental Retardation without there being a direct causal link.

Mental Retardation and Child Abuse

Students with Mental Retardation are at greater risk of being sexually, physically, or emotionally abused than other students or adolescents of the same age. Students with Mental Retardation tend to be naïve and immature and have poor intellectual and social problem-solving skills. They are therefore particularly vulnerable to all types of abuse.

Developmental Mental Retardation and Immaturity

Children and adolescents with Mental Retardation very commonly show signs of marked immaturity. Indeed, one of the diagnostic criteria for Mental Retardation is that the student not only has an IQ below 70, but also has problems in adaptive functioning. Recreational choices, ability to self-regulate behavior, and ability to act in an independent way are all likely to be delayed in students who have Mental Retardation.

Professionals Who May Be Involved

Teachers

Home teachers, regular classroom teachers, and special educators will have a primary role in supporting the student with Mental Retardation.

Psychologists

Psychologists will be involved in the formal assessment of the student's IQ and may be responsible for monitoring the student's progress over the years. Psychologists may also be involved to help manage Emotional or Behavioral Disorders that may occur concurrently or develop as a result of the student's cognitive disability.

Speech Pathologists

Speech pathologists may be involved to address some specific speech- and language-related difficulties experienced by the student.

Occupational Therapists and Physical Therapists

Occupational therapists or physical therapists may be involved in the provision of Developmental Adapted Physical Education (DAPE) for the student with Mental Retardation.

Pediatricians

Pediatricians will have an ongoing role in managing medical issues and may be involved in the treatment of Attention-Deficit Disorder.

Child Psychiatrists

Child psychiatrists may be involved to deal with emotional and behavioral issues that can arise when a student has Mental Retardation.

Disability Specialists

Disability specialists may be involved, particularly when the Mental Retardation is severe or profound. These professionals may support families in dealing with matters such as sexuality, life skills, social skills, and so forth.

Social Workers

Social workers may be involved to support the family of a student with Mental Retardation. Respite care and additional financial and practical support may be available if needed.

Community and Government Agencies

There are likely to be community and government agencies offering specific support to these students and their families.

Action Plans for Students With Mental Retardation

- Set up an assessment or reassessment plan to identify areas of specific difficulty and to isolate any areas in which the student may have aptitudes or strengths.
- Set up an individualized education program to meet the student's needs.
- Ensure that all factors that are contributing to the student's difficulties, such as problems with general medical health, hearing, eyesight, social disadvantage, and so forth, are identified and managed appropriately.
- Arrange for specialist support in areas of specific difficulty, such as speech pathology for poor language skills, DAPE for coordination difficulties, and so forth.
- Offer individual or very small group support in core areas of the curriculum. Given that students with Mental Retardation will almost certainly have substantial delays in literacy and numeracy, ensure that they receive instruction appropriate to their developmental levels.
- Ensure that the student with Mental Retardation who is in the general classroom is provided with a modified curriculum that is simplified in content.
- Provide instruction that is more explicit and is delivered at a slower pace than would usually be necessary for most students of that age.
- Offer significantly more opportunity for consolidation and practice than would normally be offered for students of that age.
- Consider that students with Mental Retardation learn less well through abstract teaching, but learn more successfully from a multisensory approach, in which they participate in the activity with hands-on learning.
- Consider the most appropriate, least restrictive class placement. The majority of students with Mental Retardation have a mild disability and are appropriately placed in a general education class with the necessary support. Students with moderate, profound, or severe Mental Retardation may be placed in special classes or schools, depending on the provisions available in their locality and, in the United States, in accordance with the requirements of IDEA.
- Ensure that the family of the student has appropriate support through school, community, and government agencies.
- Offer additional social support for those students with Mental Retardation who also have socialization difficulties. They may need explicit social skills teaching, or supported, supervised play opportunities with peers.
- Provide the student with explicit, protective behavior training to minimize the risk that he or she will be abused by others.
- Pay particular attention to transition points. For students with Mental Retardation, having a new teacher, changing classrooms, or moving

from one school to another (such as from junior high school to high school) can be very stressful. Start planning early and ensure good negotiation between all involved parties so that the transition between one learning environment and the next is as smooth as possible.

- Ensure that the student's special needs are clearly identified to visiting specialist teachers who may teach the student in a general class.
- Ensure that the student with Mental Retardation has equal opportunity to participate in a range of activities in school and out of school.
- Take into account the need for the student to be offered a program that is based on inclusion and equity of opportunity.

RECOMMENDED FURTHER READING

Commonsense Methods for Children with Special Educational Needs: Strategies for the Regular Classroom (4th Edition)
Author: Peter Westwood
Date of publication: 2002
Publisher: RoutledgeFarmer
ISBN: 0415298490

Teaching Students with Learning Problems (6th Edition)
Authors: Cecil Mercer, Ann Mercer
Date of publication: 2000
Publisher: Prentice Hall
ISBN: 013089296

The Fragile X Child
Authors: Betty B. Schopmeyer, Fonda Lowe
Date of publication: 1992
Publisher: Singular
ISBN: 1879105837

Children With Down's Syndrome: A Guide for Teachers and Learning Support Assistants in Mainstream Primary and Secondary Schools (Resource Materials for Teachers)
Author: Stephanie Lorenz
Date of publication: 1998
Publisher: David Fulton
ISBN: 1853465062

Children With Mental Retardation: A Parent's Guide (The Special Needs Collection)
Authors: Romayne Smith, Eunice Kennedy Shriver
Date of publication: 1993
Publisher: Woodbine House
ASIN: 0933149395

REFERENCES FOR MENTAL RETARDATION

AAMR Ad Hoc Committee on Terminology and Classification. (1992). *Mental retardation: Definition, classification and systems of support* (9th ed.). Washington, DC: American Association of Mental Retardation.

American Psychiatric Association. (1994). *Diagnostic and statistical manual of mental disorders* (4th ed.). Washington, DC: Author.

Beirne-Smith, M., Ittenbach, R. F., & Patton, J. R. (1998). *Mental retardation* (5th ed.). Upper Saddle River, NJ: Merrill.

Burack, J. A., Hodapp, R. M., & Zigler, E. (Eds.). (1996). *Handbook of mental retardation and development.* New York: Cambridge University Press.

Jacobson, J. W., & Mulick, J. A. (Eds.). (1996). *Manual of diagnosis and professional practice in mental retardation.* Washington, DC: American Psychological Association.

Maclean, W. E. (Ed.). (1996). *Ellis handbook of mental deficiency, psychological theory and research.* Mahwah, NJ: Erlbaum.

Sattler, J. M. (1992). *Assessment of children* (3rd ed.). San Diego, CA: Jerome M. Sattler.

Sparrow, S. S., Balla, D. A., & Cicchetti, D. V. (2000). *Comprehensive psychological and psychoeducational assessment of children and adolescents: A developmental approach.* Boston: Allyn & Bacon.

World Health Organization. (2000). *ICIDH-2: International classification of functioning, disability and health.* Geneva, Switzerland: Author.

OTHER HEALTH DISABILITIES

T his section includes three checklists:

- Attention-Deficit Disorder (Inattentive Type)
- Attention-Deficit/Hyperactivity Disorder
- Tourette's Syndrome

DEFINITION OF OTHER HEALTH IMPAIRMENT: INDIVIDUALS WITH DISABILITIES EDUCATION ACT (IDEA)

Other health impairment means having limited strength, vitality or alertness, including a heightened alertness to environmental stimuli, that results in limited alertness with respect to the educational environment, that is due to chronic or acute health problems such as asthma, Attention-Deficit Disorder or Attention-Deficit/Hyperactivity Disorder, diabetes, epilepsy, a heart condition, hemophilia, lead poisoning, leukemia, nephritis, rheumatic fever, and sickle cell anemia; and adversely affects a child's educational performance.

HOW TO USE THE CHECKLISTS

Complete the Checklist

Fill in the administrative details at the top of the form.

Consider each item in turn. Record your subjective evaluation of the extent to which that item applies to the student.

Add any additional comments or qualifications in the space provided at the end of the questionnaire.

Interpret the Checklist

The checklist is a screening instrument, and the ratings that you have selected reflect your observations of the child or adolescent. The more items that apply to a child or adolescent, and the more frequently these items have been observed, the more likely it is that the child or adolescent has the health disability indicated by the checklist that you have used. However, it is important to remember that several other conditions have similar characteristics and that specialist assessment is necessary for formal diagnosis.

For your information, descriptions of the disorders, similar conditions, and conditions that may accompany the disorders are provided.

Decide Whether to Refer for Further Assessment

The checklists will help you to decide whether to refer the student for further assessment. Guidelines are given on pages 5 and 7 for using the results of the rating scales.

Look at the Subcategories of the Checklist

The subcategories will help you isolate any specific areas of difficulty and plan appropriate intervention strategies targeted to the student's individual needs. The action plans that follow will help give you some practical ideas on intervention strategies.

THE ATTENTION-DEFICIT DISORDER
(INATTENTIVE TYPE) CHECKLIST

Glynis Hannell, BA (Hons.), MSc Registered Psychologist

Student's name _____ Date _____ Student's age _____

Name of person completing checklist _____

Relationship to student _____

Each item that applies to the child or adolescent should be checked off using the following rating scale.

0 Not at all, does not apply
1 Mild, sometimes observed, applies to some extent
2 Moderate, often observed, certainly applies
3 Severe, frequently observed, strongly applies

*Please use **0** to indicate that an item has been considered and does not apply. If the **0** is not checked, it is not clear if the item has been overlooked.*

Inattentiveness

Often seems to be daydreaming or in a world of his or her own	0	1	2	3
Sometimes says things "out of the blue" that are not relevant	0	1	2	3
Often starts things but gets distracted before he or she is finished	0	1	2	3
Often makes careless mistakes	0	1	2	3
Is sometimes suspected of having hearing problems	0	1	2	3
Often takes a very long time with everyday tasks such as dressing or eating	0	1	2	3
Often slow to respond when spoken to or asked to do something	0	1	2	3
Seems vague and unaware of what is going on	0	1	2	3

Poor organization

Often loses things that are needed for tasks or activities	0	1	2	3
Cannot organize a piece of schoolwork; does not know where to start	0	1	2	3
Does not plan ahead, leaves everything until the last minute	0	1	2	3
Seems to be unaware of urgent matters	0	1	2	3
Forgets important things	0	1	2	3
Is messy; desk, locker, school bag, etc., are always a mess	0	1	2	3
Loses important items and does not remember where they were left	0	1	2	3

Impatience

Gets easily frustrated with games or activities that need patience	0	1	2	3
Has a poor sense of time; thinks things take too long	0	1	2	3
Loses interest if things take too long	0	1	2	3

Easily distractible

Finds it hard to pay attention for long	0	1	2	3
Is easily side tracked	0	1	2	3
Starts things but does not finish them	0	1	2	3

Poor memory

Forgets instructions	0	1	2	3
Has difficulty learning by rote (e.g., times tables)	0	1	2	3

Specific learning disabilities

Has difficulties with reading or spelling	0	1	2	3
Has difficulties with writing or neatness	0	1	2	3
Is underachieving in school	0	1	2	3

Family history

Adults or other children in the family have similar traits	Yes	No	Don't Know

Additional comments and observations:

THE ATTENTION-DEFICIT/HYPERACTIVITY
DISORDER CHECKLIST

Glynis Hannell, BA (Hons.), MSc Registered Psychologist

Student's name _____ Date _____ Student's age _____

Name of person completing checklist _____

Relationship to student _____

Each item that applies to the child or adolescent should be checked off using the following rating scale.

0 Not at all, does not apply
1 Mild, sometimes observed, applies to some extent
2 Moderate, often observed, certainly applies
3 Severe, frequently observed, strongly applies

*Please use **0** to indicate that an item has been considered and does not apply. If the **0** is not checked, it is not clear if the item has been overlooked.*

Inattentiveness

Often seems to be in a world of his or her own	0	1	2	3
Sometimes says things "out of the blue" that are not relevant	0	1	2	3
Often starts things but gets distracted before he or she is finished	0	1	2	3
Often makes careless mistakes	0	1	2	3
Is sometimes suspected of having hearing problems	0	1	2	3
Takes a long time with everyday tasks such as dressing or eating	0	1	2	3
Does not seem to listen when spoken to	0	1	2	3
Seems agitated and distracted	0	1	2	3

Poor organization

Often loses things that are needed for tasks or activities	0	1	2	3
Cannot organize a piece of schoolwork; does not know where to start	0	1	2	3
Does not plan ahead, leaves everything until the last minute	0	1	2	3
Is messy; desk, locker, school bag, etc., are always a mess	0	1	2	3
Always seems to be in a muddle	0	1	2	3

Impatience

Finds it hard to wait	0	1	2	3
Is nearly always in a rush	0	1	2	3

Gets easily frustrated with games or activities that need patience	0	1	2	3
Has a poor sense of time; thinks things take too long	0	1	2	3

Impulsive

Often touches things when told not to	0	1	2	3
Acts or speaks before thinking	0	1	2	3
Repeats the same mistake over and over	0	1	2	3
Calls out in class when asked to listen or wait until asked to speak	0	1	2	3
Works too quickly and makes silly mistakes	0	1	2	3
Interrupts when others are speaking	0	1	2	3
Seems sorry for wrongdoing but does the same thing again a few minutes later	0	1	2	3

Excitable

Often gets over-excited and silly when out of routine	0	1	2	3
Does not know when to stop (e.g., with play fight or joke)	0	1	2	3
Is more excitable when tired	0	1	2	3
Loses control quickly (e.g., has tantrums over a small upset)	0	1	2	3

Easily distractible

Finds it hard to pay attention for long	0	1	2	3
Is easily side tracked	0	1	2	3
Starts things but does not finish them	0	1	2	3

Physically restless

Nearly always "on the go"; seems to have far more energy than others	0	1	2	3
Often fiddles aimlessly with small objects	0	1	2	3
Finds it hard to keep still (has to move, touch, talk)	0	1	2	3
Sometimes noisy and boisterous; sometimes disruptive in school	0	1	2	3
Finds it hard to wind down and go to sleep	0	1	2	3
Is clumsy and poorly coordinated	0	1	2	3

Social difficulties

Causes parents' friends and relatives to avoid contact because of student's active behavior	0	1	2	3
Is too difficult for babysitters to handle	0	1	2	3
Other students are cautious because of boisterous, impulsive play	0	1	2	3
Causes parents to avoid shopping trips because of difficulties managing the student	0	1	2	3
Is a poor team player; cannot wait turn; has to win; loses temper quickly	0	1	2	3

Poor memory

Forgets instructions	0	1	2	3
Has difficulty learning by rote (e.g., times tables)	0	1	2	3

Specific learning difficulties

Has difficulties with reading or spelling	0	1	2	3
Has difficulties with writing or neatness	0	1	2	3
Is underachieving in school	0	1	2	3

Early history

Was restless or overactive as a young student	0	1	2	3

Family history

Adults or other children in the family have similar traits	Yes	No	Don't Know

Additional comments and observations:

ATTENTION-DEFICIT DISORDER

Characteristics of Attention-Deficit Disorder (Inattentive Type) and Attention-Deficit/Hyperactivity Disorder

Attention-Deficit Disorder comes in two main forms, which may overlap, so that the same student may have some characteristics of both forms of the disorder or one form may be strongly predominant.

Inattentive Type

Attention-Deficit Disorder can be in an inattentive form. In this variant, students often seem to be in a daydream or "miles away." They may work very slowly and seldom finish work in the allotted time. In a classroom, they are less obvious than the hyperactive, impulsive type of student. However, they may still have substantial difficulties with their learning, because they fail to pay attention and have difficulties in sustaining effort.

Impulsive-Hyperactive Type

The more easily identified form is the impulsive-hyperactive type. Students with this form of Attention Deficit are often restless, impulsive, and loud. They tend to call out in class, find it difficult to sustain concentration, and often behave in an impulsive way. They are often easily excited and may not know when to stop, for example, continuing a play fight until it gets out of hand.

These students are often physically restless. They may find it hard to keep still, or they may be constantly touching and fiddling with things. They may run about excessively and be "on the go." They may find it hard to wind down at the end of the day and take a long time to go to sleep. Their impulsivity may lead to socialization problems and behavior problems.

Causes of Attention-Deficit Disorder

There is a strong genetic link for many students with Attention-Deficit Disorder of either form, so that very often, several members of the same family have the same type of inattentiveness.

It is sometimes felt that foodstuffs (high sugar intake, artificial colors, or other foods) are implicated in a student's inattentive behavior. Clinical studies show that there is seldom a scientifically proven link between food and concentration levels. It is therefore unlikely that a student's hyperactivity or inattentiveness is solely due to food intolerance.

Other Conditions With Characteristics Similar to Attention-Deficit Disorder

Giftedness

Intellectually gifted students may appear to have Attention-Deficit Disorder, when in fact they do not. Such students are often very quick to learn and finish tasks quickly. They may become readily bored by the slow pace and lack of challenge in a regular classroom. The more active gifted students may become disruptive. The more placid and reflective gifted students may simply drift off into their own deep and interesting inner world of thought.

Normal Developmental Stage

Many children are, simply by virtue of their developmental stage, active and impulsive. Normal children placed in a situation in which expectations exceed what is appropriate for their developmental level may appear to have Attention-Deficit Disorder when they do not. This may be particularly so when the students do not have appropriate opportunities for the healthy expression of normal energy levels and playfulness.

Emotional or Behavioral Disturbances

Students who are depressed, who are anxious, or who have behavioral difficulties may appear to have Attention-Deficit Disorder.

Epilepsy

Some forms of epilepsy can give the impression that the student is inattentive and day dreaming. Usually the episodes of apparent inattentiveness are quite brief, but they may recur very frequently.

Disorders and Difficulties That May Accompany Attention-Deficit Disorder

Attention-Deficit Disorder and Specific Learning Disabilities

There is a strong link between Specific Learning Disabilities and Attention-Deficit Disorder. Approximately 50% of students with Attention-Deficit Disorder will also have a learning disability.

Attention-Deficit Disorder and Behavioral Disturbances

Impulsive, hyperactive students may also have behavior disorders such as Oppositional Defiant Disorder and Conduct Disorder.

Professionals Who May Be Involved

Teachers

Classroom and special needs teachers will of course have a primary role in working with the student with Attention-Deficit Disorder in the school setting.

Behavior Management Specialists

Behavior management specialists may also be involved in supporting teaching staff with regard to managing inattentive and impulsive behavior.

Pediatricians

Pediatricians may offer medical support for the student with Attention-Deficit Disorder, particularly if medication is indicated.

Action Plans for Students With Attention-Deficit Disorder

- Ensure that an appropriate assessment has been made to correctly diagnose Attention-Deficit Disorder.
- Arrange a psychological assessment to eliminate the possibility that the student in the classroom is intellectually gifted and bored.
- Arrange a psychological assessment to eliminate the possibility that the student is depressed or showing signs of other forms of emotional or behavioral disorder.
- Support the parents in seeking an appropriate pediatric opinion with regard to the student's inattentiveness and possible medical options for management. Medical treatment (including medication) can be a valuable approach to Attention-Deficit Disorder. Advice with regard to this must be obtained from a pediatrician or neurologist.
- Consider using cognitive behavioral therapy to teach the students how to use self-monitoring to improve their own concentration and application.
- These students will need more reminders and more help with organizational tasks than other students. Work with parents to provide a supportive network for the students.
- In the classroom, the student with Attention-Deficit Disorder will tend to be poorly organized, inattentive, and possibly disruptive and will have difficulty staying on task. Punishments and other consequences may have little impact on their impulsive or inattentive behavior. Use positive encouragements and rewards to encourage controlled, on-task behavior. For example, make a set of reward cards that note appropriate behavior: "Well done, you started the task right away. . . . I'm proud of the way you worked until you were finished. . . . You are getting good at ignoring distractions. . . . You remembered all your equipment today—fantastic." Give these to the student and provide a small reward once a certain number of cards have been collected.
- The student with Attention-Deficit Disorder should sit near the teacher's desk, as far away from distractions as possible. Give the student specific classroom rules and clear guidelines about what is expected.
- Tasks that are short, goal focused, and active are those that can be completed the most successfully. Students with Attention-Deficit Disorder find it difficult to sustain application to tasks that take a long time to complete, require only passive listening, or do not have a specific endpoint clearly in view.
- Teach the student to watch for nonverbal cues to help him or her stay on task. Tell the students that each time you make eye contact with them, stand quietly behind them, or give some other prearranged signal, this is a reminder to concentrate on their work. This is much less disruptive to the classroom as a whole than verbal correction.
- Whispered correction is also sometimes effective. Stand very close to the student and speak only in a whisper, so that only the student can hear. Loud, angry reprimands tend to make students with Attention-Deficit/Hyperactivity Disorder much more unsettled.

- The use of a radio loop or similar device in the classroom may help the student to focus on the teacher's voice. The teacher uses a microphone (usually a small device worn around the neck), and the student uses headphones or a small receiver worn on the ear.
- Some students benefit from using headphones that transmit white noise, which blocks out distracting noises.
- To be effective, consequences must immediately follow inappropriate behavior.
- An incentive program can help modify a student's behavior, provided that the goals set are attainable and are short term.
- Allow plenty of time for students to get themselves organized, and give reminders as necessary. Allocate specific periods of time for organizational duties, for example, five minutes at the end of the school day to sort out books for homework or for the next day.
- Students with Attention-Deficit Disorder work best where a routine is well established.
- Avoid too many small pieces of equipment, materials, and so forth. It may be better to have one ring binder with all the student's workbooks inserted, rather than half a dozen or so loose books that frequently get lost or damaged.
- Structure the learning environment so that the student can attain success despite his or her difficulties. Acknowledge episodes of appropriate concentration, even if these are brief and very occasional.
- Highlight the important information in a task, and try to cut out confusing, irrelevant detail. Use colors, highlighter pens, and so forth to make the important details stand out.
- Foster self-esteem at every opportunity.
- Make sure some of the contact the student has with the teacher is positive and personal (inattentive students very often get a constant stream of criticisms and corrections).
- Provide tangible recognition of accomplishments such as badges, certificates, and so forth.
- Encourage the student to "self-talk," showing them how to talk their way through a problem: "What have I got to do?" "Where should I start?" "Have I done everything I was supposed to?"
- Brainstorm with a group of students (some of whom can organize themselves well) so that the student with Attention-Deficit Disorder can see how other people tackle handling organizational tasks, writing themselves notes, reminding themselves, planning ahead, and encouraging themselves to stay on task.
- Make sure that you have eye contact with the student before you give directions.
- When inappropriate behavior has occurred, do not ask "Why did you do that?" The student probably acted impulsively and has no logical reason for his or her actions. Simply state the rule that has been broken and talk to the student about how the problem can be resolved.

- Give the student a reason for listening to you: "If you listen carefully, you will see how easy and how much fun this is going to be."
- Make directions clear and simple, since many students with Attention-Deficit Disorder have difficulty processing a series of auditory commands.
- Small reminder notes written on the board can help the student remember what he or she has to do.
- Establish clear communication between home and school so that problems are recognized and dealt with quickly.
- Avoid making parents feel that they are to blame for their children's misbehavior in school.
- Do not expect parents to control the student's impulsive behavior at school by giving punishments and reprimands at home.
- Make sure that the student does have ample opportunity to "let off steam."
- If possible, keep to a steady routine which includes some quiet time when quiet activities are promoted.
- Make managing the student a team effort, with all adults and older siblings in the family working together in the same direction.
- Set reasonable limits and have the confidence to stick to them. (Because the students have Attention-Deficit Disorder does not mean that they can do just what they like.) Set priorities in which the student is expected to conform to expectations about very important issues. Try to ignore irritating but essentially harmless behaviors.
- Try to work with the student to develop the habit of "Stop-Think-Act."
- Students with Attention-Deficit Disorder find it hard to manage their impulses, so that instructions *not* to do something are particularly hard to follow through. They usually find it much easier to follow an instruction that tells them to do something rather than to stop doing something. Instead of saying "Don't do that," try to say, "Stand still for a second . . . look at me . . . show me your smile . . . think about your choices."

RECOMMENDED FURTHER READING

Understanding ADHD
Author: Christopher Green
Date of publication: 1998
Publisher: Ballantine Books
ISBN: 0449001520

Driven to Distraction: Recognizing and Coping with Attention Deficit Disorder from Childhood Through Adulthood
Authors: Edward M. Hallowell, John J. Ratey
Date of publication: 1995
Publisher: Touchstone Books
ISBN: 0684801280

Attention Deficit Disorders and Hyperactivity in Children and Adults
Author: Pasquale J. Accardo
Date of publication: 1999
Publisher: Marcel
ISBN: 082471962X

Attention Deficit Disorder Sourcebook: Basic Consumer Health
Information About Attention Deficit/Hyperactivity Disorder in
Children and Adults (Health Reference Series)
Author: Dawn D. Matthews
Date of publication: 2002
Publisher: Omnigraphics
ISBN: 0780806247

REFERENCES FOR ATTENTION-DEFICIT DISORDER AND ATTENTION-DEFICIT/HYPERACTIVITY DISORDER

Achenbach, T. M. (1991). *Manual for the child behavior checklist*. Burlington: Department of Psychiatry, University of Vermont.

American Psychiatric Association. (1994). *Diagnostic and statistical manual of mental disorders* (4th ed.).Washington, DC: Author.

Barkley, R. A. (1998). *Attention deficit hyperactivity disorder: A handbook for diagnosis and treatment* (2nd ed.). New York: Guilford Press.

Du Paul, G. J. (1991). Parent and teacher ratings of ADHD symptoms. *Journal of Clinical Child Psychology, 20,* 245–253.

Sparrow, S. S., Balla, D. A., & Cicchetti, D. V. (2000). *Comprehensive psychological and psychoeducational assessment of children and adolescents: A developmental approach.* Boston: Allyn & Bacon.

Taylor, M., Sandberg, S., Thorley, G., & Giles, S. (1991). *The epidemiology of childhood hyperactivity.* Oxford, UK: Oxford University Press.

Whalen, C. K., & Henker, B. (1992). The social profile of attention-deficit hyperactivity disorder: Five fundamental facets. *Child and Adolescent Clinics of North America, 1,* 395–410.

World Health Organization. (2000). *ICIDH-2: International classification of functioning, disability and health.* Geneva, Switzerland: Author.

THE TOURETTE'S SYNDROME CHECKLIST

Glynis Hannell, BA (Hons.), MSc Registered Psychologist

Student's name _____ Date _____ Student's age _____

Name of person completing checklist _____

Relationship to student _____

Each item that applies to the child or adolescent should be checked off using the following rating scale.

0 Not at all, does not apply
1 Mild, sometimes observed, applies to some extent
2 Moderate, often observed, certainly applies
3 Severe, frequently observed, strongly applies

*Please use **0** to indicate that an item has been considered and does not apply. If the **0** is not checked, it is not clear if the item has been overlooked.*

Vocal tics

Makes sudden, recurrent, rapid vocal noises (vocal tics)	0	1	2	3
Has vocal tics resembling a cough, sniff, snort, yelp, bark, grunt, or similar noise	0	1	2	3
Has vocal tics that take the form of swearing, obscenities, or repetition of words	0	1	2	3
Has vocal tics that occur at random	0	1	2	3
Has vocal tics that are involuntary and irresistible	0	1	2	3
Has vocal tics that can be temporarily suppressed with effort	0	1	2	3
Is unaware that he or she is making unusual noises	0	1	2	3

Motor tics

Makes sudden recurrent minor movements (e.g., throat clearing, blinking, sniffing)	0	1	2	3
Makes socially inappropriate movements (e.g., tongue protrusion, grimaces)	0	1	2	3
Has complex motor tics (e.g., squatting, knee bends, twirling, retracing steps)	0	1	2	3
Has motor tics that occur at random	0	1	2	3
Has motor tics that are involuntary and irresistible	0	1	2	3
Has motor tics that can be temporarily suppressed with effort	0	1	2	3
Is unaware that he or she is making unusual movements	0	1	2	3

Vocal or motor tics occur frequently and continuously

Has tics that often occur in bouts	0	1	2	3
Has tics that occur many times a day	0	1	2	3
Has tics that occur on most days	0	1	2	3
Has tics that continue for months at a time	0	1	2	3
Sometimes has periods of remission	0	1	2	3
Shows reduced severity of symptoms in late adolescence	0	1	2	3

Appears during childhood or adolescence

Began having tics between 2 and 18 years of age	Yes	No	Don't Know
Started with minor symptoms such as eye blinking	Yes	No	Don't Know
Began having tics when stimulant medication was given	Yes	No	Don't Know

Learning difficulties

Is below expectations for age and intelligence in basic literacy achievement	0	1	2	3
Is below expectations for age and intelligence in mathematical achievement	0	1	2	3

Tics change with circumstances

Experiences subdued symptoms during absorbing activities	0	1	2	3
Experiences subdued symptoms during sleep	0	1	2	3
Experiences worse tics when under stress	0	1	2	3

Obsessive-compulsive symptoms

Has compulsive behavior such as repetitive hand washing, unnecessary checking	0	1	2	3
Has compulsive thoughts such as counting, praying, repeating words silently	0	1	2	3
Has obsessional anxieties such as fear of contamination	0	1	2	3
Needs to have things in a particular order	0	1	2	3

Attention-Deficit/Hyperactivity Disorder

Is often impulsive	0	1	2	3
Is often restless	0	1	2	3
Is hyperactive at times	0	1	2	3
Has difficulties with organization	0	1	2	3
Is easily distracted	0	1	2	3

Anxiety or Depression

Tends to be anxious about minor things	0	1	2	3
Has impaired confidence because of anxiety about having tics in social situations	0	1	2	3
Sometimes seems depressed	0	1	2	3

Family history

Other members of the family have Tourette's Syndrome	Yes	No	Don't Know
Other members of the family have a tic disorder	Yes	No	Don't know

Additional comments and observations:

TOURETTE'S SYNDROME

Characteristics of Tourette's Syndrome

Tourette's Syndrome is a neurological disorder marked by spontaneous tics. In Tourette's Syndrome, both vocal and motor tics are apparent. Vocal tics may take the form of words (including swearing or repeating words), or they may be nonverbal, such as a snort, bark, or similar noise.

Motor tics are sudden minor movements such as throat clearing, touching, or tongue protrusion. Some students with Tourette's Syndrome have complex motor tics that involve squatting, deep knee bends, retracing steps, twirling, or similar nonpurposeful movements.

The motor tics are involuntary. That is, they occur spontaneously and are not deliberate. However, they do tend to be subdued when the student is absorbed in an activity, when he or she is asleep, or when the student exerts extra effort to control them.

Tourette's Syndrome usually emerges in early to middle childhood, often around 7 to 8 years of age. Stimulant medication used for Attention-Deficit/ Hyperactivity Disorder can sometimes unmask Tourette's Syndrome that was previously latent.

The student with Tourette's Syndrome may also have obsessive-compulsive symptoms. This may include compulsive behaviors, such as repetitive hand washing, or compulsive thoughts, such as repeated counting.

Causes of Tourette's Syndrome

There is a genetic component in Tourette's Syndrome. However, it can also occur spontaneously, without any previously known family history. Its basis is in a neurological dysfunction.

Other Conditions With Characteristics
Similar to Tourette's Syndrome

Anxiety Disorder

Some students with an Anxiety Disorder may develop obsessive-compulsive symptoms. That is, they may engage in repetitive hand washing, they may be anxious about cleanliness, or they may need to have things in a particular order. The differential diagnosis needs to be made by a professional with expertise in both conditions. Put simply, the difference is likely to be that the student with Tourette's Syndrome has a pattern of vocal and motor tics plus obsessive-compulsive symptoms, whereas the anxious student only has the obsessive-compulsive symptoms.

Motor Tics

Some students have motor tics that are similar to Tourette's Syndrome tics. Generally speaking, tics are more likely to occur in stressful situations, and there may be periods of time when they do not appear at all. Some students may have a tic such as a cough, facial grimace, or lip licking that is not associated with Tourette's Syndrome. The distinction is that the student either has a vocal tic or a motor tic as part of an anxiety-related tic disorder, or they have Tourette's Syndrome, but not both. In Tourette's Syndrome, both motor and vocal tics occur. An anxiety-related motor or vocal tic may disappear completely for long periods of time, particularly when the student is not stressed.

Disorders or Difficulties That May Accompany Tourette's Syndrome

Tourette's Syndrome and Attention-Deficit/Hyperactivity Disorder

Tourette's Syndrome has a strong association with Attention-Deficit/Hyperactivity Disorder.

Tourette's Syndrome and Specific Learning Disabilities

Students with Tourette's Syndrome are at greater risk of learning disorders than the general student population.

Tourette's Syndrome and Anxiety

Students with Tourette's Syndrome may become anxious because of the social implications of their condition. Anxiety and stress can increase the frequency or intensity of the vocal and motor tics. Anxiety is likely to be particularly marked when the Tourette's Syndrome symptoms are mistakenly treated as a behavioral problem and not a neurological disorder.

Tourette's Syndrome and Depression

Students with Tourette's Syndrome can readily become depressed because of the impact that their symptoms have on those around them. As with anxiety, this effect can be significantly exaggerated if the vocal and motor tics are misunderstood and treated as a behavioral problem and not a neurological disorder.

Professionals Who May Be Involved

Teachers

Teachers and special educators will all have a role in supporting the student with Tourette's Syndrome. This is particularly so if the student also has associated Attention-Deficit Disorder (with or without hyperactivity) and learning disabilities.

Pediatric Neurologists

A pediatric neurologist is of critical importance in managing Tourette's Syndrome. Medication is now available that helps to manage the vocal and motor tics in many students.

Counselors

Some students with Tourette's Syndrome may benefit from having the support of a counselor who can help the student to work through some of the issues caused by the symptoms of the disorder.

Psychiatrists

Some students with Tourette's Syndrome have significant adjustment difficulties, and these students will benefit from the support of a child or adolescent psychiatrist.

Action Plans for Children and Adolescents With Tourette's Syndrome

- Recognize that any child who presents with vocal or motor tics should be referred promptly for specialist assessment and diagnosis.
- Recognize that anxiety and stress will tend to increase the incidence of motor and vocal tics. Keep the classroom environment calm and supportive, and ensure that the student has an emotionally safe and comfortable learning and social environment at school.
- When vocal or motor tics do occur, avoid drawing attention to them. They are involuntary and spontaneous, and very difficult to control.
- Provide information and counseling for fellow students, so that they in turn can understand the nature of Tourette's Syndrome in their classmate.
- Promote good peer support and closely monitor peer group interactions to ensure that the student with Tourette's Syndrome is not harassed or discriminated against.
- Provide appropriate educational input for any learning disabilities that are apparent.
- Maintain good communication between home and school so that any minor problems are recognized quickly, before they escalate into larger problems.

RECOMMENDED FURTHER READING

**Children With Tourette Syndrome: A Parent's Guide
(Special Needs Collection)**
Authors: Tracy Haerle, Jim Eisenreich
Date of publication: 2003
Publisher: Woodbine House
ISBN: 0933149441

Coping With Tourette Syndrome and Tic Disorders
Author: Barbara Moe
Date of publication: 2000

Publisher: Rosen
ISBN: 0823929760

Taking Tourette Syndrome to School ("Special Kids in School" Series)
Author: Tira Krueger
Date of publication: 2002
Publisher: JayJo Books
ISBN: 1891383124

Tourette Syndrome
Author: Elaine Landau
Date of publication: 1998
Publisher: Franklin Watts
ISBN: 053111399X

Tourette Syndrome: The Facts
Authors: Mary M. Robertson, Simon Baron-Cohen
Date of publication: 1998
Publisher: Oxford University Press
ISBN: 019852398X

Tourette Syndrome: A Practical Guide for Teachers, Parents and Carers (Resource Materials for Teachers)
Authors: Amber Carroll, Mary Robertson
Date of publication: 2000
Publisher: David Fulton
ISBN: 1853466565

REFERENCES FOR TOURETTE'S SYNDROME

Abwender, D. A., Como, P. G., Cui, L., Kurlan, R., Parry, K., Fett, K., et al. (1996). School problems in Tourette's syndrome. *Archives of Neurology, 53,* 509–511.

Achenbach, T. M. (1991). *Manual for the child behavior checklist.* Burlington: Department of Psychiatry, University of Vermont.

American Psychiatric Association. (1994). *Diagnostic and statistical manual of mental disorders* (4th ed.).Washington, DC: Author.

Coffey, B. J., & Park, K. S. (1997). Behavioral aspects of Tourette syndrome. *Neurology America, 15,* 277–289.

Comings, D. E., & Comings, B. G. (1985). Tourette syndrome: Clinical and psychological aspects of 250 cases. *American Journal of Human Genetics, 35,* 435–450.

Walter, A. L., & Carter, A. S. (1997). Gilles de la Tourette's syndrome in childhood: A guide for school professionals. *School Psychology Review, 26,* 28–46.

World Health Organization. (2000). *ICIDH-2: International classification of functioning, disability and health.* Geneva, Switzerland: Author.

SPECIFIC LEARNING DISABILITY

There is one checklist in this section:

- Specific Learning Disability

DEFINITION OF SPECIFIC LEARNING DISABILITY: INDIVIDUALS WITH DISABILITIES EDUCATION ACT (IDEA)

The term specific learning disability means a disorder in one or more of the basic psychological processes involved in understanding or in using language, spoken or written, that may manifest itself in an imperfect ability to listen, think, speak, read, write, spell, or to do mathematical calculations, including conditions such as perceptual disabilities, brain injury, minimal brain dysfunction, dyslexia, and developmental aphasia.

The term does not include learning problems that are primarily the result of visual, hearing, or motor disabilities, of mental retardation, of emotional disturbance, or of environmental, cultural, or economic disadvantage. (Sec. 300.7)

HOW TO USE THE CHECKLIST

Complete the Checklist

Fill in the administrative details at the top of the form.

Consider each item in turn. Record your subjective evaluation of the extent to which that item applies to the student.

Add any additional comments or qualifications in the space provided at the end of the questionnaire.

Interpret the Checklist

The checklist is a screening instrument, and the ratings that you have selected reflect your observations of the child or adolescent. The more items that apply to a child or adolescent, and the more frequently these items have been observed, the more likely it is that the child or adolescent has a Specific Learning Disability. However, it is important to remember that several other conditions have similar characteristics and that specialist assessment is necessary for formal diagnosis.

For your information, descriptions of the disorders, similar conditions, and conditions that may accompany the disorders are provided.

Decide Whether to Refer for Further Assessment

The checklists will help you to decide whether to refer the student for further assessment. Guidelines are given on pages 5 and 7 for using the results of the rating scales.

Look at the Subcategories of the Checklist

The subcategories will help you to isolate any specific areas of difficulty and plan appropriate intervention strategies targeted to the student's individual needs. The action plans that follow will help give you some practical ideas on intervention strategies.

THE SPECIFIC LEARNING DISABILITY CHECKLIST

Glynis Hannell, BA (Hons.), MSc Registered Psychologist

Student's name _____ Date _____ Student's age _____

Name of person completing checklist _____

Relationship to student _____

Each item that applies to the child or adolescent should be checked off using the following rating scale.

0 Not at all, does not apply
1 Mild, sometimes observed, applies to some extent
2 Moderate, often observed, certainly applies
3 Severe, frequently observed, strongly applies

*Please use **0** to indicate that an item has been considered and does not apply. If the **0** is not checked, it is not clear if the item has been overlooked.*

Underachievement

Has difficulties in learning to read, spell, or write	0	1	2	3
Produces schoolwork that does not reflect his or her true ability	0	1	2	3
School reports say "Could do better"	0	1	2	3
Teachers think that the student is underperforming	0	1	2	3
Puts in effort not reflected in results	0	1	2	3
Only makes small improvements in response to a lot of good teaching input	0	1	2	3

Memory difficulties

Has difficulties remembering instructions	0	1	2	3
Has difficulties learning basics (e.g., letters and their sounds)	0	1	2	3
Has problems remembering words from one page to the next	0	1	2	3
Has problems learning sequences (e.g., multiplication tables)	0	1	2	3
Can learn spelling for a test but forgets the words very rapidly	0	1	2	3
Gets the sequence of letters or numbers wrong (e.g., 13 for 31, "on" for "no")	0	1	2	3
Has difficulties with arithmetic, uses fingers to count	0	1	2	3
Copies things down incorrectly	0	1	2	3
Makes the same error over and over (e.g., "whent" for "went")	0	1	2	3

Speech, phonological, and language difficulties

Has problems with "word finding" when speaking	0	1	2	3
Has problems pronouncing long words (e.g., "hostipal" for "hospital")	0	1	2	3
Has problems breaking words into sounds	0	1	2	3
Has difficulties blending sounds together	0	1	2	3
Has difficulties recognizing or producing rhymes	0	1	2	3
Has difficulties recognizing or producing alliteration	0	1	2	3
Has difficulties learning phonics	0	1	2	3
Was later than average in learning to talk	0	1	2	3
Has history of early ear infections	0	1	2	3
Is poor in structuring written language	0	1	2	3

Difficulties combining spoken and written language

Was or is slow to learn the link between sounds and letters	0	1	2	3
Can spell a word verbally but cannot write it down	0	1	2	3
Has difficulty getting thoughts on paper	0	1	2	3
Has words missing (or extra words) in written language	0	1	2	3
Reads words that are not there	0	1	2	3
Lacks fluency and speed in reading	0	1	2	3

Visual motor difficulties

Was or is slow to learn how to write	0	1	2	3
Does poor bookwork; is untidy, slow, messy	0	1	2	3
Mixes upper- and lowercase letters	0	1	2	3
Has difficulties working as fast as other students	0	1	2	3
Has poor coordination; is clumsy	0	1	2	3
Loses place when reading; uses finger to keep track	0	1	2	3
Reverses letters and numbers after the age of 7	0	1	2	3
Disliked puzzles and drawing as a younger child	0	1	2	3
Has difficulties with sustained writing; hand gets tired very quickly	0	1	2	3
Has poor posture; slumps on desk when working; fidgets sitting on the floor	0	1	2	3

Concentration difficulties

Is inattentive, in a daydream	0	1	2	3
Is easily distracted	0	1	2	3
Has been diagnosed as having Attention-Deficit Disorder	0	1	2	3
Is often restless and fidgety	0	1	2	3
Is often impulsive; does not stop and think; calls out in class	0	1	2	3

Makes many careless errors	0	1	2	3
Cannot read for more than a short period of time	0	1	2	3
Is poorly organized; often forgets books, equipment	0	1	2	3

Social and emotional difficulties

Has low self-esteem with regard to schoolwork	0	1	2	3
Avoids learning tasks; "loses" books; wastes time; "forgets" homework	0	1	2	3
Does not expect to succeed, so does not try	0	1	2	3
Gets frustrated and upset when effort does not produce good results	0	1	2	3
Is reluctant to accept help; does not like to be different	0	1	2	3
Is often told to try harder even when working very hard	0	1	2	3

Family history

Other family members have Dyslexia or similar learning difficulties	Yes	No	Don't Know

Additional comments and observations:

SPECIFIC LEARNING DISABILITY

Specific Learning Disability is also known as

- Dyslexia
- Specific Learning Difficulty
- Reading Disorder
- Disorder of Written Expression
- Mathematics Disorder
- Dyscalculia

Causes of Specific Learning Disability

There is a strong genetic component in the development of a Specific Learning Disability. At least 50% of students with a Specific Learning Disability have a first-degree relative with a similar disorder.

The difficulties with acquisition of basic skills in reading, written language, or mathematics are caused by irregularities in the way the brain processes information.

Characteristics of Specific Learning Disability

A Specific Learning Disability is marked by significant difficulties in the acquisition of basic skills in reading, written language, or mathematics. These difficulties occur despite adequate instruction and normal intelligence.

A Specific Learning Disability is due to a dysfunction in the way the student processes and retains information. This disorder often means that the student's response to appropriate intervention may be slow and inconsistent in comparison with other students who are experiencing learning difficulties due to other reasons, such as missed schooling, ill health, or inadequate instruction.

The student with a Specific Learning Disability may display significant difficulties in remembering basics that have been taught over and over. Errors may persist despite extensive amounts of instruction and practice.

Phonological difficulties may be very marked; for instance, the student may not be able to "hear" the individual sounds in a word that he or she is trying to spell.

Some students with a Specific Learning Disability may have problems with written output. Although they may be able to explain their ideas very easily when they are talking, their written language may be inaccurate, untidy, and a poor representation of what they know.

Students with Specific Learning Disabilities may have problems with mathematics as well as literacy. They may also have concentration difficulties.

Students with Specific Learning Disabilities may often become very frustrated and lose motivation because of their continual struggles with learning.

Other Conditions With Characteristics
Similar to Specific Learning Disabilities

Language Impairment

Students with a Language Impairment may appear to have a Specific Learning Disability. On thorough examination, students who have Language Impairments are found to have more global difficulties in language than students with Specific Learning Disabilities. However, there is often a very close overlap between the two conditions.

Mental Retardation

Students with limited intelligence or Mental Retardation may be suspected of having a Specific Learning Disability on the grounds that they are experiencing significant difficulties with the acquisition of basic literacy and numeracy. However, on assessment, they will be found to have general difficulties in verbal reasoning, memory, language, and perceptual reasoning. Their literacy skills may be at an appropriate level relative to their overall level of cognitive development.

Disorders or Difficulties That May
Accompany a Specific Learning Disability

Specific Learning Disability and Giftedness

A distinct subgroup of students with Specific Learning Disabilities are also intellectually gifted, or have other gifts and talents. In this situation, their general brightness may allow them to learn at an age-appropriate level and rate, so that their Specific Learning Disability may not be apparent. However, on detailed assessment, they will be found to be underachieving by a marked degree. Gifted, learning-disabled students may often be recognized by the significant discrepancy between their oral work and their reading and written work.

Specific Learning Disability and Attention-Deficit Disorder

There is known to be a significant overlap between Specific Learning Disabilities and Attention-Deficit Disorder. Approximately 60% of students with Attention-Deficit Disorder will also have a Specific Learning Disability. Approximately 30% of students with a Specific Learning Disability will also have Attention-Deficit Disorder.

In the classroom, there is likely to be a complex interaction between the underlying learning difficulty and the student's tendency to be inattentive.

Specific Learning Disability and
Depression, Anxiety, and Low Self-Esteem

The day-to-day difficulties experienced by students with Specific Learning Disabilities can make a contribution to emotional disturbance. This is particularly so if the student also has Attention-Deficit Disorder. In particular, low self-esteem may be a consequence of enduring learning difficulties and failing to achieve academically at age level.

Professionals Who May Be Involved

Teachers

Classroom teachers will have a core role in supporting students with Specific Learning Disabilities. They will modify teaching methods, curriculum materials, and assessment tasks to ensure that these students are not disadvantaged.

Special needs educators will be involved in planning and implementing an appropriate remedial program for the student with a Specific Learning Disability.

Psychologists

Psychologists with expertise in the diagnosis of Specific Learning Disabilities will provide preliminary assessment and ongoing monitoring of students.

Speech Pathologists

Speech pathologists may be involved in supporting the student, particularly with regard to phonological skills and with general issues regarding reading and written language.

Counselors, Psychiatrists, and Psychologists

Student counselors, child and adolescent psychiatrists, and child psychologists may be required to offer the student support with confidence, anxiety, and self-esteem.

Pediatricians

Pediatricians may be involved, especially if the student also has Attention-Deficit Disorder.

Organizations

Community organizations can offer support to learning-disabled students and their families and teachers. The International Dyslexia Association (http://www.interdys.org), the British Dyslexia Association (http://www.bda-dyslexia.org.uk), the Learning Disability Association of America (http://www.ldanatl.org), and the Learning Disabilities Association of Canada (http://www.ldac-taac.ca) are examples of such organizations.

Action Plans for Students With a Specific Learning Disability

- Arrange a comprehensive assessment to eliminate other, similar conditions such as a Language Impairment, Cognitive Disability, or Mental Retardation.

- Ensure that any assessment also explores the possibility that the student may be intellectually gifted, regardless of the fact that his or her school achievements are poor.
- Assess the student's particular pattern of difficulties to establish a basis for the student's Individualized Education Program (IEP). Note any special strengths as well as areas of particular difficulty.
- Develop the student's individualized learning program in consultation with the student, the student's parents, specialist educators with expertise in Specific Learning Disabilities, the student's classroom teachers, and other professionals who are involved with the student. If you are in the United States, refer to Chapter 1 to see who must be involved on the IEP team.
- Take into account the need for the student to be offered a program that is based on inclusion and equity of opportunity.
- Provide modified curriculum materials. For example, modify worksheets so that the student can read the information provided.
- Provide the support of a reader to assist the student in reading curriculum or assessment materials that have not been modified.
- Use a scribe to put the student's ideas and words into written form.
- Give abbreviated or modified assessment tasks so that the student does not have to spend an excessive amount of time on the task. Try to give the student the same workload as other students in terms of the time and effort required.
- Alter timeframes so that the student has a fair chance of completing the work successfully.
- Provide the student with ample scaffolding, such as word lists, personal dictionaries, calculators, and so forth.
- Use technology, particularly word processors.
- For students with severe Specific Learning Disabilities, explore options such as voice recognition software, text-to-speech software, and predictive word processing software. (Speech recognition software automatically types up what the student says. Text-to-speech software reads back what the student has written and will read any text loaded into the program via scanning or downloading from the Internet or disc. Predictive software predicts the next word that is going to occur in typed text, allowing the student to select a word that is grammatically correct and has accurate spelling. Predictive software may include a text-to-speech function.)
- Teach students that they may benefit from using the "autosummarize" function available in some word processing programs. This function abbreviates text (scanned or downloaded from an outside source) to a specified percentage of the original. This function highlights the key ideas to make comprehension easier.
- Remember that students may find that manually highlighting text also helps them identify the main ideas of what they are reading.
- Explore the use of software programs that organize ideas and help with "mind mapping," which are often of considerable value to the student with a Specific Learning Disability.

- Set up an appropriate remedial intervention program. The remedial program should be highly structured, taking the student through the stages of skill acquisition step by step. Plan for careful record keeping so that the program's effectiveness can be measured and regularly reviewed.
- Set timeframes for the achievement of expected learning outcomes.
- Recognize the need for constant repetition and consolidation of previously learned skills.
- Use a phonic base for the reading and spelling programs, giving the student graded instruction in the use of letters and their sounds. Respected programs include the Hickey program and the Orton Gillingham program. Programs work best under the supervision of a teacher with expertise in teaching students with a Specific Learning Disability. This teacher will draw on a range of appropriate resources to create a program that is individualized to meet a particular student's needs.
- Consider ways in which the student's motivation and confidence can be maintained, despite the fact that he or she is experiencing difficulties learning basic skills. Provide short, achievable goals, celebrate successes, and provide continuing instruction.
- Provide the student with a card stating the agreed-on special provisions so that the student is able to show this to teachers who may not be aware of the student's Specific Learning Disability.
- Make sure that students have special provisions (accommodations) when they take examinations to ensure that they have the best chance possible of demonstrating their understanding of the curriculum.

RECOMMENDED FURTHER READING

Dyslexia: Action Plans for Successful Learning
Author: Glynis Hannell
Date of publication: 2004
Publisher: Peytral (US)
ISBN: 1890455008
Publisher: David Fulton (UK)
ISBN: 1843122146

Complete Learning Disabilities Handbook: Ready-to-Use Strategies & Activities for Teaching Students with Learning Disabilities (New Second Edition)
Author: Joan M. Harwell
Date of publication: 2002
Publisher: Jossey-Bass
ISBN: 0130325627

Supporting Students With Dyslexia
Author: Hull Learning Services
Date of publication: 2004
Publisher: David Fulton
ISBN: 1843122227

Dyslexia: A Practical Guide for Teachers and Parents
Authors: Barbara Riddick, Judith Wolfe, David Lumsden
Date of publication: 2002
Publisher: David Fulton
ISBN: 1853467804

REFERENCES FOR
SPECIFIC LEARNING DISABILITY

American Psychiatric Association. (1994). *Diagnostic and statistical manual of mental disorders* (4th ed.).Washington, DC: Author.

Broomfield, H., & Combley, M. (1997). *Overcoming dyslexia: A practical handbook for the classroom*. London: Whurr.

Lyon, G. R. (Ed.). (1994). *Frames of reference for the assessment of learning disabilities*. Baltimore: Brookes.

Sattler, J. M. (1992). *Assessment of children* (3rd ed., rev. ed.) San Diego, CA: Author.

Snowling, M., & Hulme, C. (1997). *Dyslexia: Biology, cognition, and intervention*. London: Whurr.

Sparrow, S. S., Balla, D. A., & Cicchetti, D. V. (2000). *Comprehensive psychological and psychoeducational assessment of children and adolescents: A developmental approach*. Boston: Allyn & Bacon.

Turner, M. (1997). *The psychological assessment of dyslexia*. London: Whurr.

World Health Organization. (2000). *ICIDH-2: International classification of functioning, disability and health*. Geneva, Switzerland: Author.

SPEECH OR LANGUAGE IMPAIRMENT

There is one checklist in this section:

- Language Impairment

DEFINITION OF SPEECH OR LANGUAGE IMPAIRMENT: INDIVIDUALS WITH DISABILITIES EDUCATION ACT (IDEA)

Speech or language impairment means a communication disorder, such as stuttering, impaired articulation, a language impairment, or a voice impairment, that adversely affects a child's educational performance. (Sec. 300.7)

HOW TO USE THE CHECKLIST

Complete the Checklist

Fill in the administrative details at the top of the form.

Consider each item in turn. Record your subjective evaluation of the extent to which that item applies to the student.

Add any additional comments or qualifications in the space provided at the end of the questionnaire.

Interpret the Checklist

The checklist is a screening instrument, and the ratings that you have selected reflect your observations of the child or adolescent. The more items that apply to a child or adolescent, and the more frequently these items have been observed, the more likely it is that the child or adolescent has Speech or Language Impairment. However, it is important to remember that several other conditions have similar characteristics and that specialist assessment is necessary for formal diagnosis.

For your information, descriptions of the impairments, similar conditions, and conditions that may accompany the impairment are provided.

Decide Whether to Refer for Further Assessment

The checklists will help you to decide whether to refer the student for further assessment. Guidelines are given on pages 5 and 7 for using the information from the rating scales to make decisions about referral.

Look at the Subcategories of the Checklist

The subcategories will help you isolate any specific areas of difficulty and plan appropriate intervention strategies targeted to the student's individual needs. The action plans that follow will help give you some practical ideas for intervention strategies.

THE SPEECH OR LANGUAGE IMPAIRMENT CHECKLIST

Glynis Hannell, BA (Hons.), MSc Registered Psychologist

Student's name _____ Date _____ Student's age _____

Name of person completing checklist _____

Relationship to student _____

Each item that applies to the child or adolescent should be checked off using the following rating scale.

0 Not at all, does not apply
1 Mild, sometimes observed, applies to some extent
2 Moderate, often observed, certainly applies
3 Severe, frequently observed, strongly applies

*Please use **0** to indicate that an item has been considered and does not apply. If the **0** is not checked, it is not clear if the item has been overlooked.*

Late in learning to talk

Was late in learning to talk	0	1	2	3
Has needed speech therapy	0	1	2	3
Was or is slower than average to use correct grammar (e.g., "me wants," "we wented")	0	1	2	3

Difficulties with sequence of language

Finds it hard to tell a story in sequence	0	1	2	3
Finds it hard to recite nursery rhymes, times tables, days in order, alphabet	0	1	2	3
Was or is slow learning to count and recite the alphabet	0	1	2	3
Gets lost in the middle of a sentence	0	1	2	3

Word-finding difficulties

Often struggles to find the word that is needed	0	1	2	3
Uses word substitutes such as "thingy, stuff, bit"	0	1	2	3
Forgets names or words that are familiar	0	1	2	3
Puts up hand in class and then cannot remember the answer	0	1	2	3
Was or is slow to learn names of colors	0	1	2	3
Has difficulties learning names of letters or numbers	0	1	2	3

Finds it difficult to read words by sight	0	1	2	3
Is stilted and lacks fluency in reading	0	1	2	3

Not a confident talker

Is reluctant to talk to unfamiliar people	0	1	2	3
Does not usually volunteer to speak in class	0	1	2	3
Does not like to talk on the telephone	0	1	2	3

Difficulties with expressive language

Gets words mixed up (e.g., confuses "yesterday" and "tomorrow")	0	1	2	3
Gets words muddled (e.g., "I was set up" instead of "I was upset")	0	1	2	3
Has difficulties saying what he or she means	0	1	2	3
Gives up trying to explain; says "It doesn't matter"	0	1	2	3
Uses gesture, facial expressions, and mime more than others	0	1	2	3

Difficulties with receptive language

Has been suspected of having hearing difficulties even though hearing is fine	0	1	2	3
Sometimes "gets the wrong end of the stick" when listening	0	1	2	3
Does not enjoy listening to stories; prefers pictures or action	0	1	2	3
Forgets a list of instructions	0	1	2	3
Seems to be in a world of his or her own a lot of the time	0	1	2	3
Often does the wrong thing when instructions are given	0	1	2	3
Watches others for cues as to what to do in school	0	1	2	3
Often asks teacher to repeat or clarify instructions	0	1	2	3
Gets tired and "tunes out" if listening for a long time	0	1	2	3

Phonological difficulties

Had early articulation difficulties	0	1	2	3
Is poor at producing rhyming words	0	1	2	3
Is poor at producing alliteration (words with the same initial sounds)	0	1	2	3
Finds reading with phonics difficult (cannot remember sounds, cannot blend sounds)	0	1	2	3
Finds spelling with phonics difficult (cannot work out sounds in words)	0	1	2	3
Mixes up words with similar sounds	0	1	2	3

Difficulties with social language

Does not use language to solve social problems; may use physical force instead	0	1	2	3
Does not seem to understand tone of voice	0	1	2	3

Very literal; does not understand jokes, puns or metaphors, etc.	0	1	2	3
Does not use facial expression or eye contact appropriately	0	1	2	3
Is not good at turn taking in conversation	0	1	2	3
Is poor at taking the listener's needs into consideration	0	1	2	3
Talks too loudly, too softly, or too fast	0	1	2	3
Gets frustrated and upset when cannot make self understood	0	1	2	3
When upset or in trouble, cannot explain what is wrong	0	1	2	3
Forgets to use common courtesies and greetings (e.g., "Thank you," "Hello")	0	1	2	3

Problems with auditory processing

Finds it hard to hear against background noise	0	1	2	3
Is very sensitive to loud noises	0	1	2	3
Is easily distracted by noises	0	1	2	3

Additional comments and observations:

SPEECH OR LANGUAGE IMPAIRMENT

Characteristics of Speech or Language Impairment

It is important to understand the distinction between speech and language. Speech is the ability to produce sounds and articulate words. There is a normal, developmental sequence in the ability to produce specific sounds. Children with a Speech Impairment will exhibit problems in the actual pronunciation and production of words beyond the usual immaturities or irregularities that occur during the normal process of speech development. Severe problems with speech production may occur in Verbal Dyspraxia (see the Developmental Coordination and Dyspraxia section of this book).

Children or adolescents with a Language Impairment may speak very clearly but will have a disorder in the way they understand spoken or written language (receptive language) or in the way they produce their own language (expressive language).

A student who has a receptive Language Impairment will have difficulties processing the grammar or syntax of spoken or written language. He or she may misunderstand complex sentence structures and have to guess at what is being said. For example, the child may be asked "What should you do if you cut your finger?" and answer "Blood comes out." In this example, the child has picked up the simple phrase "cut your finger" and has failed to process "What should you do?"

The child with a Language Impairment may find it difficult to understand subtle differences in word use in spoken language. For example, he or she may not appreciate the difference between "Draw a line down the middle of your page," and "Draw a line to the middle of your page."

In older students, the receptive Language Impairment may take a more subtle form and may only be evident with high-order language such as reading comprehension and interpreting complex, abstract information.

An expressive Language Impairment is marked by difficulty acquiring new words, problems with word finding or word use, and the use of shortened sentences and simplified or disordered grammatical structures. The student may have trouble structuring his or her sentences correctly or may have difficulty joining sentences together to form a logical sequence.

With older students, an expressive Language Impairment may be most evident in written language.

Causes of Speech or Language Impairment

A Language Impairment is more likely to occur in children and adolescents who have a family history of similar difficulties. A Language Impairment can also be acquired through a head injury or medical condition such as encephalitis, although these are uncommon situations.

Other Conditions With Characteristics
Similar to Speech or Language Impairment

Mental Retardation

Children with Mental Retardation may appear to have a Language Impairment. The distinction between students with a Language Impairment and those with Mental Retardation is that in the case of language-impaired children, their nonverbal capacities and their adaptive skills are unimpaired. Conversely, students with cognitive disabilities will have difficulties not only in the language area, but also in the nonverbal area and with adaptive skills.

Asperger Syndrome

Some students with Asperger Syndrome may appear to have a language impairment, particularly in the social domain. A student with Asperger Syndrome may also have stilted or somewhat stereotyped language and may have trouble maintaining a dialogue with a conversational partner.

Autism

Students with Autism also have impaired language as an intrinsic part of their autistic condition.

Hearing Impairment

Students who have a Hearing Impairment will also present as having a receptive or expressive Language Impairment, due to their hearing difficulties.

Selective Mutism

Selective Mutism will also be easily mistaken for a Language Impairment. The student may be unwilling to speak at all in some situations, such as school, but be quite talkative at home. There is some evidence that Selective Mutism is sometimes associated with a subtle Language Impairment.

Disorders or Difficulties That May Accompany Speech or Language Impairment

Language Impairment and Giftedness

Students with a Language Impairment may be gifted in other areas. For instance, they may have exceptional talents in spatial, nonverbal reasoning, despite the fact that they have difficulties with language-based skills.

Language Impairment and a Specific Learning Disability

Although Language Impairment and Specific Learning Disabilities are two distinct impairments, there is an overlap between the two, particularly in the area of phonological awareness and difficulties with language structure.

Language Impairment and Attention-Deficit Disorder

Attention-Deficit Disorder is also associated with Language Impairment to a mild degree.

Language Impairment and Developmental Coordination Disorder or Dyspraxia

These conditions can be associated with a Speech or Language Impairment. Verbal Dyspraxia (difficulty with motor planning for speech) has a direct impact on expressive language skills and articulation.

Language Impairment and Anxiety

Students with Language Impairments may become anxious, particularly when they have problems with both receptive and expressive language. They may show anxiety symptoms such as being overly dependent on familiar care-givers, being somewhat socially withdrawn, or being unsettled and distressed by changes in their routine. Some children with Language Impairments develop obsessional behaviors as part of their anxiety.

Language Impairment and Socialization Difficulties

If the student has a severe Language Impairment, it is not uncommon for socialization to be impaired. Some students have a specific impairment in their social language (disorder in pragmatic language).

Professionals Who May Be Involved

Teachers

Parents, teachers, and special educators will of course have a major role in supporting the student with a Language Impairment.

Speech Pathologist

Speech pathologists are also of critical importance in providing appropriate therapy to the individual student and advisory support for teachers and parents.

Action Plans for Students
With Speech or Language Impairment

- Arrange for a comprehensive assessment to diagnose the exact nature of the Language Impairment and to eliminate other possible causes for the student's language difficulties.
- Ensure that a speech pathologist is available to provide appropriate, specialized therapy for the student.
- Ensure that teachers, special educators, support staff at school, and members of the family all have appropriate professional guidance with regard to supporting the student's developing language skills.
- Consider the possibility that a child with a significant Language Impairment may find continuous processing of language very challenging. Allow the student "language-free" periods of time during the school day to provide some respite from the demands of processing and producing language.
- Ensure that information and instructions given to the student are given in short, clear sentences, with animated facial and voice expressions and practical demonstration if possible.
- Avoid long, complex verbal explanations for a child who has a receptive Language Impairment.
- If a child has an expressive Language Impairment, allow plenty of time and offer support when talking to the child. For example, if the student

has a word-finding difficulty, first allow them plenty of unpressured time, and then give support by offering them a couple of possibilities, such as, "Was it a camel or a donkey?" If the student is trying to tell you a story but gets the order of events jumbled, ask questions such as, "How did it all start? Who was there at the beginning of the trip? What happened next?"

- There is a strong possibility that a child with a Language Impairment will have difficulties acquiring early literacy skills. Provide appropriate supplementary support if this is the case.

- Older students with a Language Impairment may have difficulties with reading comprehension and written expression. Offer extra teaching input for language-related learning. For example, offer extra help with essay writing or note-taking skills.

- Offer students alternative assessments that do not rely heavily on written or spoken language, such as a practical project in place of an essay.

- Explore options in predictive software. Students who have difficulties with written expression may benefit from using advanced software programs that predict the next word to be used and read back what has been written. Programs that help to organize ideas into a logical format can also be very helpful.

- Ensure that the student understands how to use the grammar check on the computer and that they have selected appropriate options to customize how their grammar checker works.

- A student with a Language Impairment may have some problems with social interaction because of their language difficulties. Monitor and support social and recreational activities as necessary.

RECOMMENDED FURTHER READING

Childhood Speech, Language & Listening Problems (2nd Edition)
Author: Patricia McAleer Humaguchi
Date of publication: 1995
Publisher: John Wiley & Sons
ASIN: 0471034134

Language and Communication Disorders in Children (5th Edition)
Authors: Deena K. Bernstein, Ellenmorris Tiegerman-Farber
Date of publication: 2001
Publisher: Pearson Allyn & Bacon
ISBN: 0205336353

Language Disorders From Infancy Through Adolescence: Assessment & Intervention
Authors: Rhea Paul, V. I. Paul
Date of publication: 2001

Publisher: Mosby
ISBN: 0323006604

Supporting Children With Speech and Language Difficulties
Author: Hull Learning Services
Date of publication: 2004
Publisher: David Fulton
ISBN: 1843122251

REFERENCES FOR SPEECH OR LANGUAGE IMPAIRMENT

American Psychiatric Association. (1994). *Diagnostic and statistical manual of mental disorders* (4th ed.). Washington, DC: Author.

Barrett, M. (Ed.). (1999). *The development of language.* Hove, UK: Psychology Press.

Bernstein, D. K., & Tiegerman-Farber, E. (1997). *Language and communication disorders in children.* Boston: Allyn & Bacon.

Bishop, D. V. M. (1992). The underlying nature of specific language impairment. *Journal of Child Psychology and Psychiatry, 33,* 3–66.

Bishop, D. V. M. (1998). Development of the children's communication checklist (CCC). *Journal of Child Psychology and Psychiatry, 39,* 879–891.

Klein, H. B., & Moses, N. (1999). *Intervention planning for children with communication disorders.* Needham Heights, MA: Allyn & Bacon.

Paul, R. (1995). *Language disorders from infancy though adolescence: Assessment and intervention.* New York: Mosby.

Sattler, J. M. (1992). *Assessment of children* (3rd ed., rev. ed.). San Diego, CA: Author.

Sparrow, S. S., Balla, D. A., & Cicchetti, D. V. (2000). *Comprehensive psychological and psychoeducational assessment of children and adolescents: A developmental approach.* Boston: Allyn & Bacon.

World Health Organization. (2000). *ICIDH-2: International classification of functioning, disability and health.* Geneva, Switzerland: Author.

9

OTHER SPECIAL NEEDS

This section includes five checklists:

- Giftedness
- Immaturity
- Low Self-Esteem
- Child Abuse
- Developmental Coordination and Dyspraxia

HOW TO USE THE CHECKLISTS

Complete the Checklist

Fill in the administrative details at the top of the form.

Consider each item in turn. Record your subjective evaluation of the extent to which that item applies to the student.

Add any additional comments or qualifications in the space provided at the end of the questionnaire.

Interpret the Checklist

The checklist is a screening instrument, and the ratings that you have selected reflect your observations of the child or adolescent. The more items that apply to a child or adolescent, and the more frequently these items have been observed, the more likely it is that the child or adolescent has the special need covered by the checklist. However, it is important to remember that several conditions have similar characteristics and that specialist assessment is necessary for formal diagnosis.

For your information, descriptions of the disorders, similar conditions, and conditions that may accompany the disorders are provided.

Decide Whether to Refer for Further Assessment

The checklists will help you to decide whether to refer the student for further assessment. Guidelines are given on pages 5 and 7 for using the results of the rating scales.

Look at the Subcategories of the Checklist

The subcategories will help you isolate any specific areas of difficulty and plan appropriate intervention strategies targeted to the student's individual needs. The action plans that follow will help give you some practical ideas for intervention strategies.

THE GIFTEDNESS CHECKLIST

Glynis Hannell, BA (Hons.), MSc Registered Psychologist

Student's name _____ Date _____ Student's age _____

Name of person completing checklist _____

Relationship to student _____

Each item that applies to the child or adolescent should be checked off using the following rating scale.

0 Not at all, does not apply
1 Mild, sometimes observed, applies to some extent
2 Moderate, often observed, certainly applies
3 Severe, frequently observed, strongly applies

*Please use **0** to indicate that an item has been considered and does not apply. If the **0** is not checked, it is not clear if the item has been overlooked.*

Early development

Was alert as a young infant	0	1	2	3
Walked early	0	1	2	3
Talked early	0	1	2	3
Displayed advanced language as a preschooler	0	1	2	3
Learned to read early	0	1	2	3
Early development of mathematical understanding	0	1	2	3
Showed advanced drawing skill as preschooler	0	1	2	3
Was thought to be an exceptionally bright child by preschool teachers and caregivers	0	1	2	3

High cognitive ability

Scores greater than IQ 130 on reputable intelligence scales	0	1	2	3
Scores at or above the 98th percentile on tests of intelligence or attainment	0	1	2	3
Is able to understand advanced, complex concepts	0	1	2	3
Enjoys complex games such as chess, difficult computer games	0	1	2	3
Uses and understands advanced vocabulary	0	1	2	3

Curiosity

Frequently asks insightful or innovative questions	0	1	2	3
Enjoys reading factual books, watching documentaries, visiting museums	0	1	2	3

Is not satisfied with simple answers; wants to know about a topic in depth	0	1	2	3
Likes to know how things work	0	1	2	3
Likes to invent and experiment	0	1	2	3

Advanced academic achievements

Excels in reading comprehension	0	1	2	3
Excels in math	0	1	2	3
Excels in written language	0	1	2	3

Special talents

Has outstanding artistic ability	0	1	2	3
Has outstanding musical ability	0	1	2	3
Has outstanding sporting ability	0	1	2	3
Has outstanding building/construction skills	0	1	2	3
Has outstanding leadership skills	0	1	2	3
Is a lateral or innovative thinker	0	1	2	3
Has an unusual or subtle sense of humor	0	1	2	3

Learning style

When interested, likes to spend a long time on one activity	0	1	2	3
Dislikes short, superficial tasks	0	1	2	3
Has intense interest in a particular topic (if obsessional, see Asperger Syndrome Checklist)	0	1	2	3
Catches on quickly to new work	0	1	2	3
Dislikes repetition and practice	0	1	2	3
Enjoys novelty and challenge	0	1	2	3
Tends to complicate simple tasks	0	1	2	3
Sees short cuts and wants to use them	0	1	2	3
Dislikes having to show work in math; already knows or understands the answer	0	1	2	3

Out of step with own age group

Finds own age group frustrating; prefers older friends	0	1	2	3
Prefers own company (e.g., reads in the library at recess)	0	1	2	3
Dislikes group work; prefers to work alone	0	1	2	3
Is not well understood by other children, who think he or she is weird	0	1	2	3

Academic difficulties

Has difficulties with reading, writing, or spelling (see Dyslexia Checklist)	0	1	2	3
Has difficulties with math, especially arithmetic (see Dyslexia Checklist)	0	1	2	3
Is inattentive, even when the curriculum is individualized (see Attention-Deficit Disorder checklist)	0	1	2	3
Is a perfectionist; is reluctant to make mistakes even though talented	0	1	2	3
Is reluctant to do age-level work (even with the promise of more interesting work later)	0	1	2	3
Conforms to the norm; only excels when this is expected	0	1	2	3
Is inconsistent in performance (mediocre with one teacher, brilliant with the next)	0	1	2	3

Emotional and behavioral difficulties

Understands complex adult issues and worries about them (e.g., world peace)	0	1	2	3
Does not "tolerate fools gladly"	0	1	2	3
Argues with adults; always has an answer	0	1	2	3
Uses sarcasm when speaking to peers or adults	0	1	2	3
Is easily bored and then switches off or becomes disruptive	0	1	2	3
Becomes very angry or upset with perceived unfairness (has mature sense of ethics)	0	1	2	3

Additional comments and observations:

GIFTEDNESS

Characteristics of Giftedness

Children and adolescents who have exceptional gifts or talents sometimes show these abilities very readily. They may be high-achieving students and have obvious, exceptional talents in areas such as language, literacy, music, mathematics, physical performance, spatial reasoning, art, or interpersonal skills. It is not unusual for a student to be multitalented across a wide range of areas.

However, for every obviously gifted student, there is likely to be another, equally talented student whose talents are much less obvious. The reasons for a student's high potential being hidden can include the coexistence of a disorder or difficulty such as anxiety, depression, low self-esteem, or boredom.

Some very bright students feel the need to merge with their peers and deliberately conform to the norm for their age group. Other very talented students may be stereotyped on the basis of socioeconomic, ethnic, or other criteria and may conform to the implicit and explicit expectations that are made of them because of this stereotyping.

Causes of Giftedness

Intelligence and special talents do have a genetic component. We know that intelligence, musical ability, mathematical ability, and many other human characteristics do get passed on from one generation to the next, so that having a gifted or talented parent or grandparent increases the child's chances of having similar traits. However, in no way is there a guarantee that the children will inherit special gifts or talents. Conversely, many children are born with an array of gifts and talents that are quite unexpected in terms of the aptitudes or capabilities of their parents.

The environment at home, in school, and in the community can certainly nurture and develop gifts and talents. The interaction of inborn potential and environmental forces can maximize the way exceptional potential develops and is manifested in the growing child.

Other Conditions With Similar Characteristics to Giftedness

Autism Spectrum Disorders

Students with Asperger Syndrome or Autism may have exceptional gifts in very isolated areas of skill. For instance, a student with Asperger Syndrome may have an encyclopedic knowledge about a topic of special interest, such as train timetables, types of dinosaurs, or makes of cars. It is possible for an autistic student to have an extraordinary capacity in mathematical computation, art, music, or another highly specific area.

Disorders or Difficulties That May Accompany Giftedness

Although many gifted and talented children and adolescents are happy, successful, and productive, these students are not immune to a wide range of difficulties and disorders.

Giftedness and a Specific Learning Disability

A gifted student may have a Specific Learning Disability. This will cause delay in academic development, especially in literacy and perhaps in mathematics. The underachievement caused by a learning disability may be particularly frustrating when, in other respects, the student has a very high intellectual capacity. In turn, this can readily lead to behavioral disturbances or motivational problems.

Giftedness and Language Impairment

It is possible for a student to be gifted in nonverbal areas such as spatial reasoning, music, movement, or art, but to have a Language Impairment, in which receptive or expressive language is disordered, despite the student's very exceptional capacities in other, nonverbal areas.

Giftedness and Asperger Syndrome

Asperger Syndrome can sometimes be present in the gifted student. We might see unusual or eccentric interests (typical of Asperger Syndrome) accompanied by more global brightness across a wide range of areas (typical of the gifted student).

Giftedness and Attention-Deficit Disorder

Attention-Deficit Disorder can either result in impulsive, hyperactive, and inattentive behavior or in inattentive day dreaming. Gifted students are just as likely as their less able peers to have either of these forms of inattentiveness.

A very bright student may also be incorrectly diagnosed as having Attention-Deficit Disorder in situations in which he or she is under-stimulated, bored, or frustrated.

Giftedness and Developmental Coordination or Dyspraxia

Disorders in motor planning and coordination can occur in a student who, in other respects, has remarkable gifts or talents. The difficulties may cause problems with handwriting, neatness of work, physical agility, and postural stability. There is often a marked discrepancy between such a student's oral work and his or her written work. However, in the case of Verbal Dyspraxia, the flow and organization of spoken language may also be significantly affected.

Giftedness and Emotional or Behavioral Disturbances

Very bright students may show Emotional or Behavioral Disturbances, especially if they are frustrated because their exceptional abilities are not recognized and channeled appropriately. They may experience socialization difficulties if their exceptional talents make them seem very different to the other students in a regular classroom.

The gifted student may show signs of Depression or Anxiety Disorder. Indeed, the capacity to think, understand, and analyze at an advanced level could be said to increase the student's risk of both conditions. Children and adolescents with high intellectual ability can read about, listen to, and understand information on world politics, environmental threats, terrorism, and other adult themes that can place a heavy load on their still-immature emotional and social resources.

Gifted students often have a very strong tendency toward perfectionism. In moderation, this perfectionism helps the very capable student use his or her exceptional abilities to the maximum to achieve a high level of success. In excess, perfectionism can lead the gifted student to feel depressed and anxious about his or her perceived failures in reaching perfect outcomes in performance or in life in general. Self-Esteem can be easily damaged when the perfectionist student attaches his or her sense of self-worth to achievements and then sets unachievable personal goals.

The label of giftedness can sometimes produce an adverse effect if adults forget that the student is still a normal child or adolescent who will not always perform at an optimum level. The student may still operate at an age-appropriate (not advanced) level in terms of persistence, motivation, and attitude.

Giftedness and Selective Mutism

It is by no means unknown for gifted students to also have Selective Mutism. Often perfectionists with a tendency toward anxiety, these children may only show their exceptional gifts in specific locations, such as home, but completely "close up" at school or in other less familiar settings.

Professionals Who May Be Involved

Teachers

Teachers and special educators will have a primary role to play in meeting the needs of the gifted student. Schools may offer a special program for gifted students and offer specialist teaching or mentoring for students with special gifts and talents.

Counselors

School counselors may provide emotional and social support for gifted students.

Organizations

Community organizations dedicated to supporting gifted and talented students may offer extra activities or resources for the children and adolescents and may provide support to parents.

Action Plans for Gifted Students

- Consider screening all students to identify those students who are gifted but not showing their exceptional capacities in the general classroom.
- Use both verbal and nonverbal tests to screen your students to identify those who may have exceptional talents in the visual-spatial areas.

- Arrange for a full assessment of any student thought to be showing signs of having exceptional gifts and talents (include those students who are described as exceptional at home, but not at school).
- Consider that students who may be outperforming all other students in their class may still be underperforming relative to their potential.
- Address any areas of difficulty that may be impeding the student's ability to use his or her exceptional capacities.
- Differentiate the curriculum to meet the student's particular needs.
- Replace the standard classroom curriculum with an appropriate, advanced curriculum. Successful completion of a curriculum that is already known to be below the student's interest and ability level should not be used to establish the student's right to an appropriate, advanced curriculum.
- Consider vertical age grouping, placing the gifted student alongside older students in areas in which he or she is working at an advanced level.
- Consider placing the student in a cluster group with other gifted students for extension and enrichment work in a collaborative learning environment.
- Offer additional, extracurricular activities that could offer the student additional challenges and interests, such as music, dance, art, debating, science clubs, or special interest groups.
- Consider setting up a mentoring program through which the student can meet regularly with an older student or adult with whom he or she can explore personal interests in greater depth.
- Ensure that the label of giftedness does not set up unreasonable expectations of the student. Make allowance for the fact that the student may be gifted in some areas but typical of his or her age group in others.

RECOMMENDED FURTHER READING

**Teaching Young Gifted Children in the Regular Classroom:
Identifying, Nurturing and Challenging Ages 4–9**
Authors: Sally Yahnke Walker, Elizabeth A. Meckstroth, Jargorie Lisovskis, Joan
    Franklin Smutny
Date of publication: 1997
Publisher: Free Spirit
ISBN: 1575420171

**Teaching Gifted Kids in the Regular Classroom: Strategies and
Techniques Every Teacher Can Use to Meet the Academic Needs
of the Gifted and Talented (Revised and Updated Edition)**
Editors: Susan Winebrenner, Pamela Espeland, Sylvia Rimm
Date of publication: 2000
Publisher: Free Spirit
ISBN: 1575420899, all editions

Re-Forming Gifted Education: Matching the Program to the Child
Editor: Karen B. Rodgers
Date of publication: 2002
Publisher: Great Potential
ISBN: 0910707464

REFERENCES FOR GIFTEDNESS

Colangelo, N., & Davis, G. A. (Eds.). (1997). *Handbook of gifted education.* Boston: Allyn & Bacon.

Engelsgierd, J. L. (1990). *Identifying gifted students: The gifted program handbook.* Palo Alto, CA: Dale Seymour.

Freeman, F. (1985). *The psychology of gifted children.* New York: John Wiley.

Hagen, E. P. (1980). *The identification of the gifted.* New York: Teachers College Press.

Heller, K. A., Monks, F. J., & Passow, A. H. (Eds.). (1993). *International handbook of research and development of giftedness and talent.* New York: Pergamon Press.

Sattler, J. M. (1992). *Assessment of children* (3rd ed., rev. ed.) San Diego, CA: Author.

Sparrow, S. S., Balla, D. A., & Cicchetti, D. V. (2000). *Comprehensive psychological and psychoeducational assessment of children and adolescents: A developmental approach.* Boston: Allyn & Bacon.

THE IMMATURITY CHECKLIST

Glynis Hannell, BA (Hons.), MSc Registered Psychologist

Student's name _____ Date _____ Student's age _____

Name of person completing checklist _____

Relationship to student _____

Each item that applies to the child or adolescent should be checked off using the following rating scale.

0 Not at all, does not apply
1 Mild, sometimes observed, applies to some extent
2 Moderate, often observed, certainly applies
3 Severe, frequently observed, strongly applies

*Please use **0** to indicate that an item has been considered and does not apply. If the **0** is not checked, it is not clear if the item has been overlooked.*

Play and recreation

Prefers to play with younger children	0	1	2	3
Prefers toys and activities usually enjoyed by younger children	0	1	2	3
Still enjoys stories or TV programs that were favorites when much younger	0	1	2	3
Enjoys jokes that are usually enjoyed by younger children	0	1	2	3
Continues with imaginative, make-believe play longer than most	0	1	2	3
Is more easily frightened by films or stories than most others are in own age group	0	1	2	3

Socially immature

Does not initiate friendships with own age group	0	1	2	3
Is easily intimidated by children in own age group or older	0	1	2	3
Does not initiate play with own age group	0	1	2	3
Does not join in age-group activities unless invited or encouraged	0	1	2	3
Seeks adults to sort out small upsets with peers	0	1	2	3
Is naïve and innocent for age	0	1	2	3
Is trusting and easily led	0	1	2	3
Cries readily instead of dealing with social problems	0	1	2	3
Is uninhibited; says or does things that are inappropriate for age	0	1	2	3

Was or is older than average to stop believing in Santa, Tooth Fairy, etc.	0	1	2	3
Is shy with strangers	0	1	2	3
Is less aware of current affairs than others of same age	0	1	2	3
Is less "street smart" with money than most of own age group	0	1	2	3

Dependent

Worries about separating from parents	0	1	2	3
Is unwilling to do things independently (e.g., buying a small item in a shop)	0	1	2	3
Is very dependent on one or two special friends at school	0	1	2	3
Needs a lot of reassurance from teacher with learning	0	1	2	3
Keeps very close to an adult at school recreation time	0	1	2	3
Keeps very close to an adult on family outings	0	1	2	3
Is reluctant to be left with a babysitter	0	1	2	3
Is reluctant to sleep over with a close friend or relative	0	1	2	3
Is reluctant to go on school or camp outing without a parent	0	1	2	3
Is reluctant to make simple decisions; wants adult or another child to decide	0	1	2	3
Follows the group; is unwilling to stand up for himself or herself	0	1	2	3
Is not keen to try new things (e.g., will not join a sports team without a lot of support)	0	1	2	3
Does not like to be given responsibility appropriate to age	0	1	2	3

Concentration

Concentrates less well than most of own age group	0	1	2	3
Is more playful, less able to settle to work than most of own age group	0	1	2	3
Is more physically restless in school than most others are in own age group	0	1	2	3
Is less able to handle delays than most of own age group	0	1	2	3

Academically immature

Is not up to age standard with literacy	0	1	2	3
Is not up to age standard with numeracy	0	1	2	3
Needs more adult support with learning	0	1	2	3
Does not ask for help when it is needed	0	1	2	3
Is immature in handwriting, bookwork, etc.	0	1	2	3
Shows immature organization of schoolwork	0	1	2	3
Is not good at taking the initiative in learning	0	1	2	3

Linguistically immature

Uses immature speech	0	1	2	3
Uses baby talk on occasion	0	1	2	3
Has limited general knowledge or vocabulary for his or her age	0	1	2	3
Was later than average learning to talk	0	1	2	3

Immature habits

Was late to stop sucking thumb	0	1	2	3
Was late to give up security blanket or soft toy	0	1	2	3

Physical immaturity

Has less physical stamina than other children of the same age	0	1	2	3
Has less well-developed gross motor skills	0	1	2	3
Has less well-developed fine motor skills	0	1	2	3
Is physically smaller than most of own age group	0	1	2	3
Needs more sleep than most of own age group	0	1	2	3
Appearance of first teeth was later than usual	0	1	2	3
Was slower to toilet train than others	0	1	2	3
Was late to become dry at night	0	1	2	3
Was late to reach puberty	0	1	2	3
Gets tired and tearful or cranky more quickly than most	0	1	2	3

Additional comments and observations:

IMMATURITY

Characteristics of Immaturity

Immaturity is not a disorder or disease, but it is very commonly cited as a cause for concern or given as a reason for observed behaviors or difficulties.

Children and adolescents do naturally vary in the rate at which they mature physically, cognitively, emotionally, and socially, and inevitably in any age group, some will be less mature than others.

However, in some circumstances, the child or adolescent is seen as being so immature relative to his or her age group that parents and teachers want to investigate further. Sometimes the term *immature* is used to explain characteristics that are, in fact, more correctly described as other disorders. For example, a child with an Anxiety Disorder or Mental Retardation may be described as immature.

It is rare for extreme immaturity to occur without an underlying disorder, difficulty, or disability.

Few children or adolescents are globally immature. The checklist provided can help you to determine where any apparent immaturities are evident. Sometimes this will lead to consideration of other diagnostic categories, or, under the Individuals with Disabilities Education Act in the United States, the more general category, "developmental delay."

Causes of Immaturity

There is no one cause of immaturity. Children and adolescents will naturally vary in the way they mature in matters such as emergence of language, onset of puberty, and physical development, and we all accept that there is a wide, natural variation.

Severe physical ill health can lead to delayed physical development and may also affect emotional and social development. For instance, a child with a life-threatening illness may spend many months in a hospital and be deprived of normal play, socialization, and learning opportunities. The interruption in normal development is very likely to result in delayed acquisition of a range of skills. The emotional repercussions for the child and family may mean that dependency and emotional immaturity follow from a period of ill health even when a physical recovery has been made.

Insecurity and instability can also contribute to immaturity. The child who has had an unstable pattern of caregivers and family situations, or who has been psychologically or physically abused, is unlikely to mature in the same way as a child who has been in a secure, stable, and loving environment.

Family circumstances may also contribute to overall immaturity. For instance, a child may be overprotected and treated like a younger child, so that he or she fails to develop appropriate levels of personal independence. However, it is fair to say that the child's intrinsic personality is likely to play a part. Some children elicit such treatment from adults or accept it without complaint, whereas others are highly intolerant of being held back and resist being treated as younger than they are.

Many types of immaturity are aspects of other developmental disorders, such as Language Impairment, Mental Retardation, Anxiety Disorder, and so forth.

Other Conditions With Characteristics Similar to Immaturity

As indicated in the previous sections, it is often the case that the immature student is in fact a student with a disorder or disability, often in a mild and not easily identified form. Immaturity or delay in a specific area of development can be intrinsic elements of the following categories of special need:

- Mental Retardation
- Specific Learning Disability
- Attention-Deficit/Hyperactivity Disorder
- Attention-Deficit Disorder (Inattentive Type)
- Language Impairment
- Anxiety Disorder
- Selective Mutism
- Developmental Coordination Disorder and Dyspraxia
- Conduct Disorder
- Oppositional Defiant Disorder
- Child Abuse
- Asperger Syndrome

Professionals Who May Be Involved

Teachers

The classroom teacher and possibly the special educator will have primary responsibility for supporting the immature student.

Psychologists

A psychologist with expertise in the diagnosis of childhood difficulties and disorders should provide a comprehensive assessment of the student to ensure that the observed immaturities are not, in fact, symptomatic of an underlying disorder or disability.

Social Workers, Counselors, Psychiatrists, and Psychologists

A social worker, counselor, or psychiatrist may be involved in supporting the family in the provision of developmentally appropriate opportunities to enable the student to mature to an appropriate level.

Action Plans for Immature Students

- Arrange for a comprehensive assessment to eliminate the possibility that the immaturity is a symptom of an underlying disorder or difficulty. In many situations, what is first thought to be immaturity proves to be another disorder such as an impairment in language, cognitive development, or emotional development.

- Look at the pattern of immaturities indicated in the checklist. Select those areas in which no immaturity was noted and take steps to develop and enhance those areas.
- Some immaturities are simply attention-seeking devices. Ensure that the student receives attention for mature behaviors and that immature behavior, if possible, gets no response.
- Some immaturities occur because the student has not developed appropriate problem-solving skills and is overly dependent on others when difficulties are encountered. Model and teach appropriate problem-solving strategies.
- Look at the areas in which immaturities were indicated, and select those that cause most disadvantage to the student or concern to the adults. Take each characteristic and provide further detail. For example, if you have checked, "Does not like to be given responsibility appropriate to age," give examples of occasions when this has occurred. List responsibilities that the student will accept and those that he or she typically rejects. This will give you and others a clearer picture of the areas of difficulty.
- Develop a plan in consultation with parents and appropriate specialists to address the specific immaturities noted. Plan to give the student graduated, nonthreatening opportunities to extend what he or she can do.
- Arrange for the student's family to receive appropriate counseling if the parenting style or family circumstances seem to be delaying appropriate levels of maturity.
- Do not force an immature student to move too far out of his or her comfort zone, as negative pressure and anxiety will tend to increase rather than reduce dependency.

RECOMMENDED FURTHER READING

Raising an Emotionally Intelligent Child
Author: John Gottman
Date of publication: 1998
Publisher: Fireside
ISBN: 0684838656

Kids Are Worth It
Author: Barbara Coloroso
Date of publication: 2002
Publisher: Harper Resource
ISBN: 0060014318

7 Strategies for Developing Capable Students
Authors: Stephen Glenn and Michael Brock
Date of publication: 1998

Publisher: Prima Lifestyles
ISBN: 0761513566

**Parents Do Make a Difference: How to Raise Kids With Solid
Character, Strong Minds and Caring Hearts**
Author: Michele Borba
Date of publication: 1999
Publisher: Jossey-Bass
ISBN: 0787946052

Using Picture Story Books to Teach Children Character Education
Author: Susan Hall
Date of publication: 2000
Publisher: Oryx Press
ISBN: 1573563498

REFERENCES FOR IMMATURITY

Berger, K. S. (2001). *The developing person through the life span.* New York: Worth.

Berk, L. E. (1999). *Child development.* Needham Heights, MA: Allyn & Bacon.

Damon, W., Kuhn, D., & Siegler, R. S. (Eds.). (1998). *The handbook of child psychology* (5th ed.). New York: John Wiley & Sons.

Das, J. P., Naglieri, J., & Kirby, J. (1994). *Assessment of cognitive processes.* Boston: Allyn & Bacon.

Einfield, S. L., & Tonge, B. J. (1992). *Manual for the developmental checklist: Primary carer version.* Sydney, Australia: School of Psychiatry, University of New South Wales.

Kamphaus, R. W., & Frick, P. J. (1996). *The clinical assessment of child and adolescent personality and behavior.* Needham Heights, MA: Allyn & Bacon.

Light, P. (1986). *The development of social sensitivity.* Cambridge, UK: Cambridge University Press.

Rholes, W. S., Blackwell, J., Jordan, C., & Walters, C. (1980). A developmental study of learned helplessness. *Developmental Psychology, 16,* 616–624.

Sparrow, S. S., Balla, D. A., & Cicchetti, D. V. (2000). *Comprehensive psychological and psychoeducational assessment of children and adolescents: A developmental approach.* Boston: Allyn & Bacon.

THE LOW SELF-ESTEEM CHECKLIST

Glynis Hannell, BA (Hons.), MSc Registered Psychologist

Student's name _____ Date _____ Student's age _____

Name of person completing checklist _____

Relationship to student _____

Each item that applies to the child or adolescent should be checked off using the following rating scale.

0 Not at all, does not apply
1 Mild, sometimes observed, applies to some extent
2 Moderate, often observed, certainly applies
3 Severe, frequently observed, strongly applies

*Please use **0** to indicate that an item has been considered and does not apply. If the **0** is not checked, it is not clear if the item has been overlooked.*

Unrealistic perceptions about self

Often says negative things about himself or herself	0	1	2	3
Sometimes exaggerates or fabricates stories to inflate his or her image	0	1	2	3
Does not expect to be liked	0	1	2	3
Does not expect to succeed	0	1	2	3

Weak foundations for positive self-esteem

Has learning difficulties	0	1	2	3
Has social difficulties	0	1	2	3
Is clumsy and poor at physical skills	0	1	2	3
Comes from a family with low self-esteem	0	1	2	3

Not confident with schoolwork

Is unwilling to try new things unless sure of success	0	1	2	3
Does not initiate own learning	0	1	2	3
Seldom takes on extra or more challenging tasks	0	1	2	3
Does not volunteer answers in class	0	1	2	3

Does not cope well with failure

Often says "I don't know" or "I can't remember," rather than make an error	0	1	2	3
Gets upset if he or she loses	0	1	2	3

Argues things are not fair when he or she fails	0	1	2	3
Will not have another try once he or she has failed at something	0	1	2	3
Attributes failures to bad luck	0	1	2	3
Exaggerates failures when they do occur	0	1	2	3
Is very readily embarrassed	0	1	2	3
Is reluctant to ask for help when in difficulty	0	1	2	3
Devalues the success of others	0	1	2	3

Does not cope well with success

Brags and "goes over the top" when he or she has succeeded	0	1	2	3
Is uncomfortable with praise or compliments	0	1	2	3
Minimizes successes when they do occur	0	1	2	3
Attributes success to good luck	0	1	2	3

Finds it hard to accept responsibility for own actions

Denies wrongdoing even when clearly at fault	0	1	2	3
Unwilling to make decisions for himself or herself	0	1	2	3
Gives credit to others when things go well	0	1	2	3
Finds it difficult to apologize	0	1	2	3

Negative perceptions from others

Is frequently put down by siblings	0	1	2	3
Is frequently put down by peers	0	1	2	3
Is often put down by adults in family	0	1	2	3
Is often put down by adults at school	0	1	2	3
Is often a victim of teasing or bullying	0	1	2	3

Easily led

Is anxious to follow peer group fads and fashions	0	1	2	3
Is easily led by others	0	1	2	3
Does not initiate activities	0	1	2	3
Does not voice own opinion	0	1	2	3

Image is very important

Tries to look tough	0	1	2	3
Tries to maintain a "cool" image	0	1	2	3
Tries to impress peers by acting clownish in school	0	1	2	3
Acts tough even though unsure of himself or herself	0	1	2	3
Relies on possessions to gain prestige	0	1	2	3

Does not have positive friendships

Tends to bully younger or weaker children	0	1	2	3
Associates with peers who are unpopular with others	0	1	2	3
Often tries to buy friendships	0	1	2	3

Eating patterns disturbed

Tries to improve image by extreme dieting	0	1	2	3
Uses food for comfort	0	1	2	3

Additional comments and observations:

LOW SELF-ESTEEM

Characteristics of Low Self-Esteem

Low self-esteem is apparent when the student places a low value on his or her own self-worth. The student may feel that he or she is not as good as others in the school, community, or family. Students may feel inadequate and less deserving of being loved or liked. They may feel less entitled to fairness and equal opportunity than others. Students with low self-esteem usually have low self-confidence. In the classroom, such students may be anxious about failure, so that they anticipate difficulties and approach tasks with reluctance.

Although success and achievement are important parts of self-esteem, it is important to remember that self-esteem relates not only to what you can do, but to who you are and how much that is valued by yourself and others.

Students with low self-esteem often feel that they have little control or power over their daily lives and that they have to be passive victims of whatever life serves up to them. They are often reluctant to volunteer to participate and unwilling to take the initiative in learning, play, or socialization.

Some students with low self-esteem may brag and act in an attention-seeking way in an attempt to impress their peers and disguise their feelings of inadequacy.

Causes of Low Self-Esteem

Some children do seem to be born with a predisposition to a negative mind-set and low self-esteem, whereas others are more inclined to have naturally positive, confident outlooks. There is likely to be a genetic component in this variation in intrinsic temperament and personality.

Parenting and family style will also impact a student's self-esteem. Negative role models of low self-esteem from older siblings and adults can affect a developing child's sense of his or her own self-worth in the family or community.

Negative life experiences can have a significant impact on a student's self-esteem. Being sexually, physically, or emotionally abused can have a major impact on a student's sense of self-worth. Experiencing difficulties with concentration, learning, or socialization can also have a damaging effect on a student's self-esteem.

Other people's behavior can contribute to the student's loss of self-esteem. A parent or teacher may be constantly and inappropriately critical; siblings or peers may harass, ridicule, tease, and put the student down.

Other Conditions With Characteristics Similar to Low Self-Esteem

Depression

Depression and low self-esteem are very closely connected and there is often significant overlap. If Depression is the primary underlying disorder, then self-esteem can be expected to improve once Depression has been treated or has spontaneously resolved.

Disorders or Difficulties That May Accompany Low Self-Esteem

Low Self-Esteem and Specific Learning Disabilities

Students who experience significant difficulties with learning despite the fact that they are intellectually just as bright as their peers may lose self-esteem through continued difficulties and failures in the classroom.

Low Self-Esteem and Attention-Deficit Disorder

Students with Attention-Deficit Disorder may be inattentive in the classroom, their impulsive behavior may often get them into trouble in the schoolyard and at home, and they may perform poorly in school. Constant criticism and correction can erode their sense of self-esteem.

Low Self-Esteem and Child Abuse

Low self-esteem may contribute to a child being selected as a victim by an abuser. A child or adolescent with a low sense of his or her own value will be less likely to be assertive and more likely to remain silent when abuse occurs. Loss of self-esteem is also a very common consequence of being sexually, physically, or mentally abused.

Low Self-Esteem and Depression

These two conditions can coexist or can mimic each other. Expert clinical judgment is required to diagnose and treat the student who has symptoms of Depression and low self-esteem.

Professionals Who May Be Involved

Teachers

Teachers will have the primary duty of care for a student with low self-esteem. Teachers with expertise in Emotional and Behavioral Disturbances may offer special programs to help the student with self-affirmation, self-respect, and appropriate social skills.

Counselors

School counselors may offer the student with low self-esteem personal counseling and support.

Social Workers

Social workers will be involved in cases in which the student has been abused or comes from a dysfunctional family.

Psychiatrists and Psychologists

Child and adolescent psychologists and psychiatrists may be consulted if the low self-esteem is severe and needs special treatment.

Action Plans for Students With Low Self-Esteem

- Plan to deal with any causal factors that are contributing to the student's low self-esteem, such as:

  inappropriate treatment at home (excessive punishment, abuse, constant criticism),

  inappropriate treatment at school (teasing, harassment), or

  inappropriately managed learning or behavioral difficulties.

- Provide your students with a positive role model by consistently treating individual differences and needs with acceptance and respect.
- Create a positive, confident atmosphere in your classroom. Make it a place where all students share in a sense of pride in belonging to that particular class.
- Teach teamwork and interdependence so that all students' unique contributions are valued.
- Make sure that all of the students in your room are encouraged to respect each other and appreciate the diversity of attributes that exist within the group of students.
- Use biographies, literature, and guest speakers from your community to show the students that every individual has a unique contribution to make to his or her community.
- Reward positive personal qualities as well as academic achievements.
- Make discipline strategies positive and respectful. Give the student ownership of a problem and support him or her in resolving it.
- Ask rather than tell. Convey a positive view of the student, not a negative one: "I'll bet you can tell me which rule you forgot," instead of, "You knew that you were not allowed over there and what did you do? You went straight over there!"
- Make explicit reference to a student's positive qualities in your daily exchanges: "Jack, I can always trust you," or "Maria, you're the tops, you just keep on trying."
- Tell your students how you feel about them: "I'm impressed," "I'm so proud of you," and "It's great to see you back." Remember that your body language speaks as loudly as your words.
- Make praise specific so that the student knows that it is genuine and related to something that has really happened.
- Praise effort and attitude rather than outcomes. Not every student can write a great story, but every student can give his or her best effort.
- Provide opportunities for the student to feel that he or she can contribute and have something to offer. Showcase the student's strengths.
- Arrange for appropriate assessment and treatment if the student appears to be depressed.

RECOMMENDED FURTHER READING

Promoting Positive Thinking
Author: Glynis Hannell
Date of publication: 2004
Publisher: David Fulton
ISBN: 184312257X

Raising Confident Boys: 100 Tips for Parents and Teachers
Author: Elizabeth Hartley-Brewer
Date of publication: 2001
Publisher: Perseus
ISBN: 1555613209

**Stick Up for Yourself: Every Kid's Guide to Personal
Power & Positive Self-Esteem**
Author: Gershen Kaufman
Date of publication: 1999
Publisher: Free Spirit
ISBN: 1575420686

The Confident Child: Raising Children to Believe in Themselves
Author: Terri Apter
Date of publication: 1998
Publisher: Bantam
ISBN: 0553379860

**Self-Esteem Games: 300 Fun Activities That Make Children Feel Good
About Themselves**
Author: Barbara Sher
Date of publication: 1998
Publisher: John Wiley & Sons
ISBN: 0471180270

**200 Ways to Raise a Girl's Self-Esteem: An Indispensable Guide for
Parents, Teachers & Other Concerned Caregivers**
Author: Will Glennon
Date of publication: 1999
Publisher: Conari Press
ISBN: 1573241547

Your Child's Self-Esteem
Author: Dorothy Briggs
Date of publication: 1988
Publisher: Main Street Books
ISBN: 0385040202

**Changing Behavior: Teaching Children With Emotional and
Behavioral Difficulties in Primary and Secondary Classrooms**
Authors: Sylvia McNamara, Gill Moreton
Date of publication: 1995
Publisher: David Fulton
ISBN: 1853463507

REFERENCES FOR LOW SELF-ESTEEM

Baumeister, R. F. (Ed.). (1993). *Self-esteem: The puzzle of low self-regard.* New York: Plenum Press.

Bracken, B. A. (Ed.). (1996). *Handbook of self-concept: Developmental, social and clinical considerations.* New York: John Wiley & Sons.

Coopersmith, S. (1967). *The antecedents of self-esteem.* San Francisco: W. H. Freeman.

Damon, W., Kuhn, D., & Siegler, R. S. (Eds.). (1998). *The handbook of child psychology* (5th ed.). New York: John Wiley & Sons.

Harter, S. (1982). The perceived competence scale for children. *Child Development, 53,* 87–97.

Hattie, J. A. (1992). *Self-concept.* Hillsdale, NJ: Lawrence Erlbaum.

Osborne, R. E. (1996). *Self: An eclectic approach.* Boston: Allyn & Bacon.

Piers, E., & Harris, D. (1969). *The Piers-Harris children's self-concept scale.* Nashville, TN: Counselor Recordings & Tests.

Sparrow, S. S., Balla, D. A., & Cicchetti, D. V. (2000). *Comprehensive psychological and psychoeducational assessment of children and adolescents: A developmental approach.* Boston: Allyn & Bacon.

Whylie, R. C. (1989). *Measures of self-concepts.* Lincoln: University of Nebraska Press.

THE CHILD ABUSE CHECKLIST

Glynis Hannell, BA (Hons.), MSc Registered Psychologist

Student's name _____ Date _____ Student's age _____

Name of person completing checklist _____

Relationship to student _____

Each item that applies to the child or adolescent should be checked off using the following rating scale.

0 Not at all, does not apply
1 Mild, sometimes observed, applies to some extent
2 Moderate, often observed, certainly applies
3 Severe, frequently observed, strongly applies

*Please use **0** to indicate that an item has been considered and does not apply. If the **0** is not checked, it is not clear if the item has been overlooked.*

Explicit sexual behavior

Engages in sexually explicit play; makes sexually explicit comments, jokes, etc.	0	1	2	3
Sees a sexual meaning in everything	0	1	2	3
Draws attention to own body or private parts	0	1	2	3
Masturbates inappropriately	0	1	2	3
Overly interested in bodily functions such as urination, menstruation, etc.	0	1	2	3
Develops a crush (with sexual overtones) on a teacher or older student	0	1	2	3
Tells untrue stories about sexual encounters with unlikely people	0	1	2	3
Seems uninhibited; will approach strangers inappropriately	0	1	2	3

Withdrawn behavior

Seems remote and "switched off"	0	1	2	3
Seems sullen and uncommunicative	0	1	2	3
Seems tired and unwilling to work or play	0	1	2	3
Does not want to talk or write about himself or herself (e.g., will not write vacation journal)	0	1	2	3
"Blocks" personal questions (e.g., "can't remember" what he or she did during the weekend)	0	1	2	3
Refuses or is anxious to go to school; does not want to leave parent	0	1	2	3

Is secretive at home or at school	0	1	2	3
Often wants to go to the medical room or be taken home	0	1	2	3

Social difficulties

Is overly possessive of one or two friends	0	1	2	3
Rejects friendship when it is offered	0	1	2	3
Tries to buy friends	0	1	2	3
Is erratic; is friendly one day, unfriendly the next	0	1	2	3
Is bad tempered and easily annoyed by small things	0	1	2	3
Is verbally and physically aggressive when upset	0	1	2	3

Deterioration

Does worse schoolwork than previously	0	1	2	3
Displays a more negative attitude toward learning	0	1	2	3
Is less willing to take risks and is more anxious about failure	0	1	2	3
Is less easygoing socially	0	1	2	3
Takes less pride in self and achievements	0	1	2	3
Is less well behaved than previously	0	1	2	3
Changes eating patterns (eats too much or too little)	0	1	2	3
Has regressed to thumb sucking, soiling, bed wetting, etc.	0	1	2	3

Moody, emotional behavior

Cries very readily	0	1	2	3
Seems irritable and cranky	0	1	2	3
Is unnecessarily apologetic and ingratiating	0	1	2	3
Makes poor eye contact	0	1	2	3
Is very clingy to adult or special friend	0	1	2	3
Wants a lot of reassurance	0	1	2	3
Is obsessional (e.g., about cleanliness or neatness)	0	1	2	3
Seems angry and defiant	0	1	2	3
Harms self (e.g., self-inflicted cuts, burns)	0	1	2	3
Engages in very risky behavior	0	1	2	3
Attempts suicide	0	1	2	3

Other disorders are apparent

Seems to have very low self-esteem (see Low Self-Esteem Checklist)	0	1	2	3
Shows signs of depression (see Depression Checklist)	0	1	2	3
Shows signs of conduct disorder (see Conduct Disorder Checklist)	0	1	2	3

Signs of distress in artwork or writing

Depicts angry, violent, or tragic themes in artwork	0	1	2	3
Produces very restrained, cautious, timid artwork	0	1	2	3
Bases written stories on angry, violent, or tragic themes	0	1	2	3
Produces sexually explicit drawings or stories	0	1	2	3

Physical injury

Has unexplained bruises, burns, etc.	0	1	2	3
Is unwilling to undress for swimming, physical education, etc.	0	1	2	3
Takes frequent days off school	0	1	2	3
Makes frequent visits to the lavatory	0	1	2	3
Has frequent urinary tract infections	0	1	2	3

Family history

Other family members have been abused	Yes	No	Don't Know
Protection or supervision of child questionable	Yes	No	Don't Know

Additional comments and observations:

THE ABUSED CHILD OR ADOLESCENT

Characteristics of the Abused Child or Adolescent

A student may be abused physically, emotionally, or sexually. This abuse can take place in the home, the neighborhood, or the school. Typically, the student who is being abused feels powerless and may even feel ashamed and worthless. The student may feel fearful about reporting the abuse for a range of reasons. The student may fear that he or she will not be believed or even will be blamed for what is happening, or that he or she will receive further abuse for speaking out, or that he or she may get a parent or other adult in serious trouble.

Sudden changes in a student's mood and behavior can signal that abuse is occurring. The student may seem moody, withdrawn, and depressed. There may, of course, be obvious bruises or marks if the abuse is physical. The student may avoid situations in which these marks can be observed or may have vague explanations of how they acquired these marks. Some students may stay away from school until bruises have faded.

Emotional and sexual abuse is often more difficult to detect, and they are generally marked by negative mood and behavior. Some students express their experiences in artwork or writing that has negative, violent, or explicit content, but often the student's response is to try to block out any reference to the abuse that is occurring. The sexually abused student may display inappropriate sexual behavior toward other students or adults.

Many abused students have a sense of pessimism about the future and may be clinically depressed.

Causes of Child Abuse

Child abuse is a complex social issue; the distinction between abuse and culturally sanctioned adult behavior toward children and adolescents can be a difficult one to make in some situations. However, it is generally agreed that adult behavior that neglects, harms, or could harm the physical, emotional, or social well-being of a child or an adolescent is abusive.

Many cases of abuse stem from adults who themselves have disorders or dysfunctions that impair their ability to deal with the child or adolescent appropriately. However, these adults are still subject to the laws that prohibit child abuse and are liable to receive severe penalties when abuse occurs.

Other Conditions That Have
Characteristics Similar to Child Abuse

Depression

Depressed students often have behavior patterns quite similar to those shown by abused students, such as being withdrawn, negative, and uncommunicative.

Conditions That May Accompany Child Abuse

Child Abuse and Depression

Many abused students are depressed as a consequence of the abuse that they have suffered. Depression may continue for a long time after the abuse has stopped.

Child Abuse and Attention-Deficit/Hyperactivity Disorder

Students with Attention-Deficit/Hyperactivity Disorder are more prone to being abused than other students. There may be other family members who also have Attention-Deficit/Hyperactivity Disorder and the combination of an impulsive, emotionally labile adult and a demanding, impulsive, and inattentive child or adolescent may create an environment conducive to emotional and physical abuse.

In school and other group settings, the student with Attention-Deficit/ Hyperactivity Disorder may trigger inappropriate responses in adults if these adults lack training or expertise in managing challenging behaviors.

Child Abuse and Mental Retardation

Students with intellectual impairments are more vulnerable to sexual abuse than most other students because of their naïveté and poor social judgment.

Professionals Who May Be Involved

Teachers

All developed countries have legislation to ensure that children and adolescents are protected from abuse by adults. This generally means that professionals such as teachers have a mandatory duty to report cases of known or suspected child abuse to the appropriate authority. Teachers will be responsible for supporting the abused student in school academically, socially, and emotionally.

Child Protection Team

Usually there will be a child protection team (social worker, psychiatrist, psychologist, legal adviser) available to offer the student ongoing counseling and support. Family members may also be in need of counseling and support for themselves from the child protection team. Legal professionals will also be involved if the case becomes the subject of court action.

Alternative Caregivers (Foster Parents)

Foster parents or other caregivers may become key adults if the abused child or adolescent is removed from an abusive home.

Action Plans for the Abused Child or Adolescent

- Remember that you are almost certainly required by law to report any situation in which you suspect that child abuse has occurred. Usually you must report your suspicions to an authority that has responsibility for child protection, not just to your colleagues or school administration. Often, however, you may be expected to work through your senior colleagues or administration to process your report and forward it to the appropriate authority. Check the reporting procedure of your school or organization and the statutory authority and make sure that you have followed all the required steps.

- Document your concerns in detail and keep your records secure. If you have reported your concerns directly to the statutory authority, advise your senior colleagues and administration of your actions.
- If appropriate, discuss your concerns with the student's parents, but make it clear that you have a legal obligation to report your concerns to the appropriate authority.
- Teach all students appropriate protective behaviors so that they have a clear idea of what they should do in potentially abusive situations. Generally, these programs include:

discussing how the students can recognize potentially abusive situations;

teaching the students about their rights to feel safe and to be safe;

training the students in assertive, self-protective behaviors;

discussing contingency plans for reporting abuse, such as identifying a trusted adult to tell;

providing the telephone number of a reputable helpline;

assuring the students that they will be believed if they report abuse;

assuring students that they will not be in trouble for reporting abuse; and

encouraging students to support each other in resisting and reporting abuse.

- Students who are being (or who have been abused) may well show emotional or behavioral disturbances, so ensure that the classroom environment is as supportive, consistent, and nurturing as possible.
- Work as a team with the child's social worker, psychologist, psychiatrist, and parent or caregiver to ensure that there is a network of support for the student.
- The general classroom teacher is in a unique position to observe the student day by day. Monitor the student's emotional and social well-being and continue to report matters of concern to the appropriate professionals.
- Refer to the Action Plans for Students With Depression section of this book (p. 59).
- Refer to the Action Plans for Students With Low Self-Esteem section of this book (p. 155).

RECOMMENDED FURTHER READING

Child Abuse: Betraying a Trust (Information Plus Reference)
Author: Mei Ling Rein
Date of publication: 2003
Publisher: Information Plus
ISBN: 0787660698

Child Abuse and Neglect: The School's Response
Authors: Connie Burrows Horton, Tracy K. Cruise
Date of publication: 2001
Publisher: Guilford Press
ISBN: 1572306734

Recognizing Child Abuse: A Guide for the Concerned
Author: Douglas J. Besharov
Date of publication: 1990
Publisher: Free Press
ISBN: 002903082X

Understanding Child Abuse and Neglect (5th Edition)
Author: Cynthia Crosson-Tower
Date of publication: 2001
Publisher: Pearson Allyn & Bacon
ISBN: 0205337953, all editions

REFERENCES FOR CHILD ABUSE

Besharov, D. J. (1990). *Recognizing child abuse: A guide for the concerned.* New York: Free Press.

Cichetti, D., & Cohen, D. J. (Eds.). (1995). *Developmental psychopathology: Risk, disorder and adaptation.* New York: John Wiley & Sons.

Corby, B. (1993). *Child abuse: Towards a knowledge base.* Buckingham, UK: Open University Press.

Damon, W., Kuhn, D., & Siegler, R. S. (Eds.). (1998). *The handbook of child psychology* (5th ed.). New York: John Wiley & Sons.

Elliott, M. (1992). *Protecting children: Training pack for front line carers.* London: HMSO.

Goddard, C. R. (1996). *Child abuse and child protection: A guide for health, education and welfare workers.* Melbourne, Australia: Pearson Professional.

Oates, R. K. (Ed.). (1990). *Understanding and managing child sexual abuse.* Sydney, Australia: Harcourt Brace Jovanovich.

Rogers, W. A., Hevey, D., & Ash, E. (Eds.). (1989). *Child abuse and neglect: Meeting the challenge.* London: BT Batsford and Open University.

Walker, C. E., Bonner, B. L., & Kaufman, K. L. (1988). *The physically and sexually abused child: Evaluation and treatment.* New York: Pergamon Press.

Wattam, C. (1992). *Making a case in child protection.* Harlow, UK: Longman.

Wiehe, V. R. (1992). *Working with child abuse and neglect.* Itasca, IL: F. E. Peacock.

THE DEVELOPMENTAL COORDINATION DISORDER AND DYSPRAXIA CHECKLIST

Glynis Hannell, BA (Hons.), MSc Registered Psychologist

Student's name _____	Date _____ Student's age _____
Name of person completing checklist _____	
Relationship to student _____	

Each item that applies to the child or adolescent should be checked off using the following rating scale.

0 Not at all, does not apply
1 Mild, sometimes observed, applies to some extent
2 Moderate, often observed, certainly applies
3 Severe, frequently observed, strongly applies

*Please use **0** to indicate that an item has been considered and does not apply. If the **0** is not checked, it is not clear if the item has been overlooked.*

Delay in physical development

Was delayed in achieving physical milestones (sitting, crawling, walking)	0	1	2	3
Was late to establish hand dominance (left or right handed); swaps hands	0	1	2	3

Delay in self-care skills

Was late in learning to dress/undress; has trouble with buttons, buckles, laces	0	1	2	3
Needs help to get arms in sleeves or legs into trousers	0	1	2	3
Gets clothes inside out or the wrong way around	0	1	2	3
Was slow to learn to use a knife and fork	0	1	2	3
Is a messy eater compared with others of the same age	0	1	2	3

Gross motor difficulties

Is clumsy or accident prone	0	1	2	3
Takes a long time and effort to master a physical skill (e.g., hopping or skipping)	0	1	2	3
Finds it hard to imitate someone else's movements	0	1	2	3
Looks awkward when running	0	1	2	3
Has poor timing of physical responses (e.g., finds it hard to catch a ball)	0	1	2	3

Avoids playground equipment or moving toys	0	1	2	3
Is reluctant to take part in physical activities (e.g., team games or competitive sports)	0	1	2	3

Poor muscle tone

Has difficulties in holding own weight on climbing bars	0	1	2	3
Slouches at the table; finds it hard to sit up straight	0	1	2	3
Sprawls on school desk when working	0	1	2	3
Has poor posture when walking	0	1	2	3
Finds it difficult to sit still on the floor	0	1	2	3

Poor balance

Is poor at balancing (e.g., on a wall or beam)	0	1	2	3
Falls over easily; bumps into things	0	1	2	3
Was or is late learning to ride a bike	0	1	2	3

Poor fine motor coordination

Has difficulties using scissors	0	1	2	3
Often drops or spills things	0	1	2	3
Accidentally breaks things by holding too tight	0	1	2	3
Has an abnormal pencil grip; often changes grip	0	1	2	3
Presses too hard when writing	0	1	2	3
Forms letters incorrectly; uses several strokes instead of a continuous line	0	1	2	3
Has difficulties sustaining neat writing; starts well but quickly becomes messy	0	1	2	3

Visual-spatial difficulties

Has a verbal IQ that is substantially higher than performance IQ	0	1	2	3
Is slow to copy from the board or inaccurate in copying	0	1	2	3
Is poor at puzzles or construction activities	0	1	2	3
Has underdeveloped drawing skills for age group	0	1	2	3
Is messy in bookwork; starts in the wrong place; has poor spacing	0	1	2	3
Has a poor sense of direction	0	1	2	3

Speech and language difficulties

Was late in learning to talk	0	1	2	3
Speech is unclear or words come out wrong	0	1	2	3
Finds it hard to express himself or herself, especially if upset or tired	0	1	2	3

Under- or overreaction to sensory information

Is easily overwhelmed by loud noises or crowded places	0	1	2	3
Dislikes unfamiliar sensations (e.g., textures, smells)	0	1	2	3
Does not like to be touched	0	1	2	3
Does not like to be swung or moved unexpectedly	0	1	2	3
Needs a high level of sensory input (always tapping, fidgeting, etc.)	0	1	2	3

Family history

Siblings or other family members have difficulties with coordination	Yes	No	Don't Know

Additional comments and observations:

DEVELOPMENTAL COORDINATION DISORDER AND DYSPRAXIA

Characteristics of Developmental Coordination Disorder and Dyspraxia

There is significant clinical discussion with regard to whether Developmental Coordination Disorder and Dyspraxia are one and the same disorder or two similar but separate disorders. The terms are often used interchangeably.

It is important to note that Developmental Coordination Disorder and Dyspraxia are not necessarily due to low muscle tone. Although low muscle tone can be part of the problem, the more central difficulty is usually one of motor planning difficulties in the brain's neurological circuits. Difficulties that relate only to poor muscle development usually respond rapidly to appropriate practice (the muscle physically builds up and the problem is resolved). For most students with Developmental Coordination Disorder or Dyspraxia, the difficulties are much less easily remedied, because the problem is neurological, not muscular.

Students can have verbal Dyspraxia. This means that the motor planning required for speech is dysfunctional in some way. This may often mean that words come out wrong or that the student's speech lacks fluency.

Some students with Developmental Coordination Disorder or Dyspraxia also have sensory integration difficulties. These students find it difficult to process incoming sensory information effectively. As a result, they may be over- or under-sensitive to smell, touch, noise, or movement. They may also be "hungry" for sensory input, so they constantly create a high level of sensory input for themselves by touching, tapping, fidgeting, and so forth.

Causes of Developmental Coordination Disorder and Dyspraxia

The connection between the brain's centers that plan an action and the muscle groups in the body that implement this action is highly complex. In some students and adolescents, there is an irregularity or a dysfunction in the way the messages from the brain are formulated, transmitted to the muscle groups, and followed through in action. This can result in clumsy gross or fine motor movement. There is often a strong family history with regard to the condition. Some students who have general developmental delay may prove to have ongoing difficulties with coordination.

Other Conditions With Characteristics Similar to Developmental Coordination Disorder and Dyspraxia

Mental Retardation

A distinction should be made between students whose overall development is delayed (cognition, language, motor skills) and those who have a specific delay in coordination. The latter group may have Developmental Coordination Disorder, and the previous group (global difficulties) may be presenting with Mental Retardation with coordination difficulties as part of the general delay in development.

Speech Impairment

Students with a Speech or Language Impairment may be late learning to talk, and their speech may be unclear or may lack fluency.

Disorders or Difficulties That May Accompany Developmental Coordination Disorder and Dyspraxia

Developmental Coordination Disorder or Dyspraxia and Speech and Language Impairment

There is thought to be a mild association between Language Impairment and Developmental Coordination Disorder and Dyspraxia.

Developmental Coordination Disorder or Dyspraxia and Mental Retardation

Students with Mental Retardation may also have Developmental Coordination Disorder.

Professionals Who Are Likely to Be Involved

Occupational Therapists and Physical Therapists

Occupational therapists and physical therapists will be likely to offer appropriate intervention and treatment programs for students who are presenting with either fine or gross motor difficulties.

Speech Pathologists

Speech pathologists will be involved in the management of a student's verbal dyspraxia.

Teachers

Teachers will provide overall support for students with Developmental Coordination Disorder or Dyspraxia.

Action Plans for Students With Developmental Coordination Disorder or Dyspraxia

- It is important to have an accurate, comprehensive assessment, to indicate the types of problems the student is experiencing.
- It is important to recognize that Developmental Coordination Disorder and Dyspraxia are neurological problems that will not necessarily be fixed

by simply providing additional practice. What you see in the student's work may be the outcome of years of practice, therapy, and effort.

- Difficulties with coordination and neatness can be very frustrating. Avoid asking the student to try harder or do better. They may be doing the best that they can already, and extra effort will not necessarily produce any improvements at all.

- Students may find maintaining a good sitting posture on the floor very difficult, so provide appropriate seating.

- Coordination difficulties will almost certainly flow through to difficulties with neatness. Graphics, diagrams, and handwriting may be very untidy. Do not penalize the student for this. Encourage the student to use alternatives such as photocopies, photographs, computer-generated graphics, and so forth.

- Coordination difficulties will often mean that the student can only write for a few minutes at a time before neatness deteriorates. Allow extra time and plenty of rest breaks when sustained writing is essential. Do not penalize the student for untidy writing.

- Avoid giving unnecessary copying to do. For instance, provide copies of class notes and worksheets in which most of the work is already set out and all the student has to do is fill in the critical pieces of information.

- The student may have significant difficulties with the speed of written work. Give the student extra time or an abbreviated task. Allow extra time in tests and examinations. Give dictation, spelling, and other tests on an individual basis so that the student does not get left behind if the class test goes more quickly than he or she can write.

- Students with handwriting problems may need to use a computer as their primary means of written communication.

- Some students with Developmental Coordination Disorder find typing difficult. They may need to work with a scribe or use voice recognition software to produce written language.

- Students who get overwhelmed by too much sensory input may need special consideration, such as being given extra support at a very noisy or crowded event.

- Students may need something tactile (a small ball, a string of beads, a piece of dough) to manipulate to keep up a steady flow of sensory input.

- The student may need a modified curriculum, particularly in areas in which physical coordination is required. For instance, in sports, games, gymnastics, and so forth, the student's special needs may need to be identified and a differentiated curriculum offered.

- Teachers and specialists working with the student may consider the use of special aids, such as a sloping writing surface and easy-to-grip pens.

- Students may need to be taught and reminded to use good posture when doing deskwork (feet on the floor, chair well tucked in to support the back).

- Provide plenty of opportunities to develop physical coordination through fun activities (sport, arts and crafts, outdoor activities, etc.).

RECOMMENDED FURTHER READING

Children With Developmental Coordination Disorder:
Strategies for Success
Author: Cheryl Missiuna
Date of publication: 2001
Publisher: Haworth Press
ISBN: 0789013584

Motor Coordination Disorders in Children
Author: David A. Sugden
Date of publication: 1998
Publisher: Sage
ISBN: 0761909990

Developmental Coordination Disorder
Author: Sharon A. Cermak
Date of publication: 2001
Publisher: Singular
ISBN: 0769300928

Helping Children With Dyspraxia
Author: Maureen Boon
Date of publication: 2001
Publisher: Jessica Kingsley
ISBN: 1853028819

Dyspraxia in the Early Years: Identifying and Supporting
Children With Movement Difficulties
Author: Christine M. Macintyre
Date of publication: 2000
Publisher: David Fulton
ISBN: 1853466778

Inclusion for Children with Dyspraxia: A Handbook for Teachers
Author: Kate Ripley
Date of publication: 2001
Publisher: David Fulton
ISBN: 1853467626

Dyspraxia: A Guide for Teachers and Parents
(Resource Materials for Teachers)
Author: Kate Ripley
Date of publication: 1997
Publisher: David Fulton
ISBN: 1853464449

Childhood Speech, Language & Listening Problems (2nd Edition)
Author: Patricia McAleer
Date of publication: 2001
Publisher: John Wiley & Sons
ISBN: 0471387533

Developmental Dyspraxia—Identification and Intervention:
A Manual for Parents and Professionals
Author: Madeleine Portwood
Date of publication: 1999
Publisher: David Fulton
ISBN: 1853469882

REFERENCES FOR DEVELOPMENTAL COORDINATION DISORDER AND DYSPRAXIA

American Psychiatric Association. (1994). *Diagnostic and statistical manual of mental disorders* (4th ed.). Washington, DC: Author.

Chu, S. (1996). Evaluating sensory integration functions of general school children with specific developmental disorders. *British Journal of Occupational Therapy, 59*(10), 465–474.

Daly, S. (1992). Understanding dyspraxia. *Nursing Times, 88*(30), 38–39.

Dewey, D., & Wison, B. (2001). Developmental coordination disorder: What is it? *Physical and Occupational Therapy in Pediatrics, 52*(3), 88–92.

Gueze, R. H., Jongmans, M. J., Schoemaker, M., & Smits-Engelsman, B. C. (2001). Clinical and research criteria for developmental coordination disorder: A review and discussion. *Human Movement Science, 20*(1), 7–47.

Henderson, S. E., & Barnett, A. L. (1998). The classification of specific motor coordination disorders in children: Some problems to be solved. *Human Movement Science, 17,* 449–469.

Hill, E. L. (1998). A dyspraxic deficit in specific language impairment and developmental coordination disorder: Evidence from hand and arm movements. *Developmental Medicine & Child Neurology, 406*(6), 388–395.

Miller, L. T., Missiuna, C. A., Macnab, J. J., & Malloy-Miller, L. T. (2001). Clinical description of children with developmental coordination disorder. *Canadian Journal of Occupational Therapy, 68*(1), 5–15.

Miyahara, M., & Mobs, I. (1995). I. Developmental dyspraxia and developmental coordination disorder. *Neuropsychology Review, 5*(4), 245–268.

Polatajko, H. J., Mandich, A. D., Miller, L. T., & Macnab, J. J. (1995). An international consensus on children with developmental coordination disorder. *Canadian Journal of Occupational Therapy, 62*(1), 3–6.

Ripley, K., Daines, B., & Barrett, J. (1998). *Dyspraxia: A guide for teachers and parents.* London: David Fulton.

WARNING SIGNS OF SENSORY IMPAIRMENT

This section contains two lists for sensory impairments:

- Hearing Impairment
- Visual Impairment

WARNING SIGNS OF HEARING IMPAIRMENT

A Hearing Impairment may occur in only one ear, or it may exist only at certain frequencies. For instance, a child may hear low sounds quite clearly but have difficulties with high-frequency sounds (or vice versa), so that what they hear is broken up by gaps where a specific frequency loss occurs. For instance, they may hear "Sue is going to have a shower" as "Ue i going to have a ower," but hear "Mom will help you do the job," quite clearly.

- Has trouble hearing when two or more people are talking.
- Appears to have trouble hearing when there is a lot of background noise.
- Frequently misunderstands you when you speak.
- Asks you to repeat what you have said.
- Watches your face intently when you are speaking.
- Responds inappropriately to what others are saying.
- Seems in a world of his or her own at times.
- Speech is unclear or immature. May have trouble with sounds at a specific frequency.

- Grammar is incorrect or immature.
- Has the television sound turned up high.
- Sits very close to the teacher or the television.
- Tilts head to listen.
- Mouths the words as others speak.
- Has had recurrent ear infections.
- Seems to switch off when listening in a group.
- Speaks more loudly than is necessary.
- Watches others and copies them when instructions are given.
- Does not respond to speech when not able to see the speaker.
- Sits close to the front when given the choice.

For a checklist of developmental abilities from birth through age 5, see "How Does Your Child Hear and Talk?" from the American Speech-Language-Hearing Association (http://www.asha.org/public/speech/development/child_hear_talk.htm).

WARNING SIGNS OF VISUAL IMPAIRMENT

A Visual Impairment can occur in one or both eyes. Some children who wear eyeglasses still cannot see as well as other students, because prescription lenses may not necessarily be capable of restoring perfect vision.

- Eyes do not coordinate; one moves in a different direction from the other.
- Eyes move excessively.
- Often blinks.
- Often rubs eyes.
- Often has infections, red eyes, or crusted lids.
- Eyes water very easily.
- Has difficulty learning to read.
- Holds books very close.
- Puts head very near the desk when working.
- Tilts head to one side when writing or drawing.
- Loses place when reading or copying; skips lines.
- Leaves words out when reading or copying.
- Confuses colors.
- Has very poor posture when reading or writing.
- Squints, frowns, or leans forward when copying from the board.
- Copies from students sitting nearby instead of copying from the board.
- Copies things incorrectly; confuses similar shapes such as 3 and 8.
- Moves head excessively when reading.
- Sits very close to the television or board.
- Has messy bookwork.
- Complains of headaches.
- Complains of difficulties seeing clearly.

Index

**CORWIN
PRESS**

The Corwin Press logo—a raven striding across an open book—represents the union of courage and learning. Corwin Press is committed to improving education for all learners by publishing books and other professional development resources for those serving the field of PreK–12 education. By providing practical, hands-on materials, Corwin Press continues to carry out the promise of its motto: **"Helping Educators Do Their Work Better."**